J. Robert Oppe...
Biography on t...
Bomb and His En... ...Ethics, and Nuclear Physics

by
J.R. MacGregor

*This book is dedicated to my dear father
without whose support I could have never succeeded.*

Copyright © 2023 1359906 B.C. LTD.

All rights reserved.

No portion of this book may be reproduced in any form without written permission from the publisher or author, except as permitted by U.S. copyright law.

ISBN: 978-1-950010-61-5

Table of Contents

Table of Contents..3
Prologue...5
   Rise of Quantum Physics...8
Introduction..17
Chapter 1 Family...20
Chapter 2 Growing Up...27
   Early Struggles..33
Chapter 3 Star of Academia..36
   The Oppenheimer-Philips Process....................................43
Chapter 4 Jean Tatlock...46
Chapter 5 Katherine Oppenheimer..55
Chapter 6 Manhattan Project...62
   First Nuclear Reactor...68
   Building Chicago Pile-1...70
   Hanford Site and Oak Ridge..73
   Enrichment Challenges..74
   Thin Man..76
   Setbacks..77
   Little Boy...79
   Fat Man..81
   Trinity..82
Chapter 7 Bombings...86
   Aftermath and Significance...88
   Legacy and Ethical Implications of the Manhattan Project....90
Chapter 8 His Philosophy & Atoms for Peace........................92
   Nuclear Activism...97
   The Acheson-Lilienthal Report: Pioneering International Control of Atomic Energy...98
   Oppenheimer's Urgent Plea for Nuclear Diplomacy............100
Chapter 9 Betrayed...103
   Consequences...110
Chapter 10 Ascent to the Stars...116
   Nobel Prize..119

Conclusion..122
    The Luminary's Legacy: Shaping Science Education..........124
    A Moral Imperative: Scientists as Guardians of Wisdom.....128
    Oppenheimer's Many Scientific Contributions.....................131
    J. Robert Oppenheimer in Popular Culture: A Multi-Faceted Portrait...138
    A Tapestry of Interpretation and Myth...............................140
        Ethical Evolution..142
        Myth vs. Reality..143
    A Human Who Changed History...144

Prologue

"A person who never made a mistake never tried anything new."
Albert Einstein

In the late 19th and early 20th centuries, the world of science underwent a remarkable transformation. This era, known for its breathtaking discoveries, set the stage for the scientific revolution that was to unfold. At the heart of it all was a deep-seated belief in classical physics, a framework established by the brilliant mind of Sir Isaac Newton, which had held sway for centuries.

Classical physics, inspired by Newton's groundbreaking principles of motion and gravity, had successfully unraveled the mysteries of the visible world. It provided a comprehensive understanding of how objects move, how planets orbit the sun, and how forces govern our interactions with the physical universe. With its laws serving as a reliable guide for explaining everyday phenomena, classical physics seemed invincible.

However, there were cracks in this seemingly unassailable fortress of knowledge. Classical physics struggled to make sense of certain puzzling observations. One glaring issue that puzzled scientists, but was oblivious to the rest of the world was something called blackbody radiation.

Blackbody radiation refers to the electromagnetic radiation emitted by an idealized object called a "blackbody" that absorbs all incident radiation and emits it again in thermal equilibrium. Blackbodies are theoretical constructs that do not exist in reality, but they serve as a useful model for understanding the behavior of radiation from objects at different temperatures.

According to classical physics, radiation of this kind should intensify to infinity as temperatures rise. This conundrum, known as the "ultraviolet catastrophe," challenged the limits of classical physics and signaled the need for new insight and ways of looking at matter and forces.

This was the beginning, for as scientists probed further, they encountered another inconsistency: the behavior of particles at incredibly small scales and high speeds. Classical and Newtonian physics, which had been so effective on a larger scale, faltered colossally when it was applied to subatomic particles. This signaled a need for a revolutionary approach, a new way of thinking about the fundamental building blocks of our universe.

This call for change gave rise to quantum mechanics, a revolutionary perspective of this facet of nature that ended up shattering the foundations of classical physics. Energy and subatomic particles could now be understood better, and with that better understanding, the path to mastering nuclear power, among other things, began to be paved.

In the wake of this scientific awakening, physicists such as Max Planck and Albert Einstein would make significant contributions to the evolving notions of the time. Max Planck's bold proposition that energy was quantized – existing in discrete packets called "quanta" – paved the way for a deeper understanding of light and matter. Albert Einstein further expanded on this notion, explaining the photoelectric effect and revealing that light could behave both as particles and waves.

The implications of these ideas were astounding. Louis de Broglie subsequently introduced the concept of wave-particle duality, suggesting that all matter could exhibit both wave-like and particle-like behaviors. This marked a departure from the solid, deterministic world of classical physics into the hazy, uncertain realm of the quantum universe.

Erwin Schrödinger's wave equation and Niels Bohr's model of the atom added to the growing chorus of quantum voices. They proposed that particles were described by complex wave functions, and electrons within atoms occupied quantized energy levels, bringing order to the chaos at the atomic scale.

However, even as quantum mechanics began to provide answers, it also ignited debates and philosophical dilemmas about the nature of reality itself.

Amidst these debates, one name resonated: Albert Einstein. While he made significant contributions to quantum mechanics, he remained skeptical of its principles. He famously exclaimed, "God does not play dice with the universe," expressing his unease with the probabilistic nature of quantum phenomena as opposed to the neat order of classical physics.

In this dynamic landscape of shifting paradigms, a clear realization emerged: classical physics, while mighty, was not infallible. And quantum mechanics emerged as a revolutionary next step forward, offering insights into the hidden workings of the micro-world.

Rise of Quantum Physics

Diving deep into this scientific revolution, we find Max Planck at the forefront, an audacious thinker who dared to challenge conventional wisdom. In 1900, Planck unveiled his quantum theory of radiation, a seismic departure from the continuous and predictable world described by classical physics. He proposed that energy, rather than being a continuous flow, was quantized into discrete packets called "quanta," as mentioned above. And this bold idea laid the cornerstone for a new way of understanding light and matter.

Yet, it was Albert Einstein who would propel these quantum seeds into full bloom. In 1905, he illuminated the perplexing photoelectric effect with a revelation that upended centuries-old notions. He proposed that light consisted of discrete particles, or photons, each carrying a distinct quantum of energy. This revelation not only explained the photoelectric effect but also shattered the boundary between particles and waves, opening a portal to an uncharted realm.

But this dual nature of light, both particle and wave, was not to be confined to photons alone. Louis de Broglie ventured further, extending the concept of duality to matter itself. In 1923, he postulated that particles like electrons could exhibit both wave-like and particle-like behaviors, depending on the circumstances. This audacious proposal challenged the very foundations of deterministic classical physics, introducing a new layer of uncertainty into the scientific narrative.

As these quantum pioneers danced on the precipice of the unknown, Erwin Schrödinger entered the stage with a revolutionary number of his own. In 1926, Schrödinger introduced his wave equation, a mathematical masterpiece that described the behavior of quantum particles as wave functions. This groundbreaking equation breathed life into the concept of probability waves, painting a picture of particles existing in a realm of uncertainty until measured.

While Schrödinger's waves propagated through the scientific community, another figure stepped into the spotlight – Niels Bohr. With Bohr's atomic model in 1913, the enigmatic dance of electrons within atoms found an elegant choreography. Bohr introduced the notion of quantized energy levels, explaining the discreet lines observed in atomic spectra. These quantum leaps were not just a fanciful display but the rhythm of an intricate quantum dance.

The emergence of quantum mechanics was beyond the shadow of a doubt a tectonic shift, a seismic departure from the classical traditions that had held sway for centuries. The predictable clockwork of Newton's world yielded to a dance of uncertainty, where particles pirouetted between states and waves whispered tales of probability. And so quantum mechanics grew, giving rise to a new narrative of reality—one that would shape the course of scientific exploration.

Louis de Broglie's wave-particle duality revelation was one that seemed to defy the boundaries of human intuition. It suggested that particles, those fundamental building blocks of matter, could exhibit dual behaviors—simultaneously manifesting as particles and as waves. This concept shattered the dogmas of classical physics that had clung to the security of fixed definitions.

Imagine, if you will, a cosmic ballet where electrons, those elusive inhabitants of atoms, waltzed in harmonious ambiguity. Electrons, traditionally understood as particles following predictable paths, were now reimagined as intangible waves, their positions described by complex probabilities rather than concrete certainties. This notion was as paradoxical as it was liberating, opening a Pandora's box of inquiries into the true essence of reality.

This dance of duality did not confine itself to the abstract realms of quantum mechanics. Its echoes resounded across the landscapes of imagination and experimentation, leaving scientists grappling with perplexing questions. Could something be both here and there, both particle and wave, existing in states of uncertainty until observed? This uncertainty would become a hallmark of the quantum realm—a realm that was transforming from a scientific curiosity into a new way of thinking about the very nature of existence.

As this new reality dawned, it beckoned a cadre of brilliant minds to contemplate its implications. The mere act of observing, it seemed, held the power to shape the universe. This realization would lay the groundwork for future explorations, igniting debates and spawning theories that sought to pierce the veil of quantum mystery.

Alluding to our earlier point, Schrödinger's wave equation, introduced in 1926, was more than a mere equation; it was a portal into the hitherto uncharted territories of the quantum realm. This equation elegantly described the behavior of particles not as fixed points in space but as probability distributions, entwining mathematics with uncertainty in a dance of profound insight.

Bohr's model of the atom helped shine a light in this era of uncertainty. It was a model that dared to embrace the dual nature of particles—those elusive electrons that wove a dance around the nucleus. Rather than fixed paths, Bohr proposed that electrons occupied quantized orbits, each orbit corresponding to a specific energy level. These orbits became the stages upon which electrons performed their mesmerizing routines.

As an electron transitioned between these orbits, a spectacle of light unfolded. Each transition emitted or absorbed a photon of precise energy, giving rise to the intricate patterns of spectral lines observed in laboratories across the world. The emission and absorption spectra of elements, once a puzzle, now found a harmonious explanation within Bohr's framework.

And then Niels Bohr and the Copenhagen interpretation of quantum mechanics, a theoretical framework named after the city that was home to his Institute of Theoretical Physics, became a guiding star for many explorers of this new realm. This idea suggested that until observed, all particles exist in a superposition of states. And when observed, they appear as a definite state. The very act of observation was now intrinsically linked to the behavior of the observed—a concept that challenged the intuitive notions of reality.

But there were also many other elements that joined the show.

Quantum numbers, for one, each assigned to an electron, defining its energy, orbital shape, orientation, and spin. These quantum numbers painted a vivid portrait of an electron's quantum state—a portrait that mirrored the intricate choreography of the quantum world.

In this world of probabilities and quantized states, Bohr's model established a bridge between the theoretical and the observed. It offered explanations for the mysteries of atomic behavior, a framework to decipher the bewildering array of spectral lines, and a glimpse into the secret lives of electrons. The model wasn't without its limitations, yet its elegance and utility ignited a fire of exploration that would continue to blaze for years to come.

Bohr's quantum dance transformed the once-murky realm of atomic physics into a stage illuminated by the light of understanding. It prepared the scientific community to embrace the realm of uncertainty, to fathom the cryptic language of quantum numbers, and to perceive the interplay between theory and experiment as an intricate ballet of knowledge.

Yet, even amidst this breathtaking choreography, debates raged. Einstein's skepticism toward the probabilistic nature of quantum mechanics continued to cast shadows across the luminous landscape. He, alongside fellow scientists like Boris Podolsky and Nathan Rosen, questioned whether the theory was truly complete, highlighting the challenges posed by what they termed "entanglement." This was what they called the mysterious phenomenon where particles separated by vast distances could instantaneously influence each other's states, defying classical notions of causality and propelling quantum mechanics into the realms of philosophy and mystique. Encapsulated in the Einstein-Podolsky-Rosen, or EPR, paradox, their challenges resonated like a philosophical thunderclap. They had constructed a thought experiment that sought to expose the apparent paradoxes within quantum mechanics. They argued that the theory's reliance on entanglement—that particles separated by vast distances could instantaneously affect each other's states—challenged the very foundations of causality and locality.

On the other end, Niels Bohr responded with equal fervor. He contended that the paradox was a manifestation of the limitations of classical intuitions when applied to the quantum world. He championed the idea that quantum systems were fundamentally indeterminate until measured, erasing the concept of objective reality prior to observation.

The debates that ensued were not just academic exercises; they were philosophical inquiries into the nature of reality itself. Could the world truly be described by the determinism of classical physics, or were we faced with a universe where uncertainty and chance held sway? Could seemingly separate particles instantly communicate their states, in defiance of the limits of space and time? These questions reached beyond equations and laboratories, tapping into the very essence of human understanding.

In the midst of the quantum revolution, a hushed realization settled in: the existing theories were both a triumph and a doorway to uncharted territories. As the dance of particles and waves grew more intricate, scientists recognized the need for a new symphony—a grand unification that could harmonize the seemingly discordant realms of quantum mechanics and relativity.

The existing theories, while shedding light on the enigmatic microcosm of particles, were fragmented. Quantum mechanics described the behavior of the infinitesimally small, while Einstein's theory of relativity elegantly explained the cosmic fabric on grand scales. Yet, as the dance between these theories intensified, the seams between them began to fray. The tiniest particles seemed to defy the fabric of spacetime, leaving scientists grappling with an unfinished puzzle.

Thus began the quest for new theories—a clarion call sounded by the unresolved questions of the quantum world. The deep undercurrents of uncertainty, wave-particle duality, and entanglement propelled thinkers to seek a theory that could elegantly weave together these disparate threads.

The need for a grand unification had reverberated through academia, calling for minds that could bridge the conceptual chasm between the minuscule and the immense. Einstein, with his bold intuition, attempted to craft a unified field theory—an endeavor to merge the forces of electromagnetism and gravity into a single framework. While his attempts would remain unfinished, they sparked the imaginations of those who followed.

As the torch passed from one generation to the next, quantum field theory emerged from the fires of human ingenuity as a contender for the coveted unification. It proposed that the fabric of reality was woven by fields—energy-filled regions that permeated space. These fields could harbor particles, and interactions between particles were understood as exchanges of field quanta. This theory, born from the fusion of quantum mechanics and special relativity, stood as a testament to the power of synthesis in scientific thought.

Yet, despite these strides, the path to a comprehensive theory remained filled with challenges. The dance of particles and fields, once again, led to conceptual problems. The delicate mathematics of quantum field theory brought forth infinities and ambiguities, casting shadows on its elegance. The endeavor to untangle these complexities led to the development of renormalization techniques—a process akin to refining a masterpiece, chiseling away imperfections to reveal a more exquisite form -- what physicists refer to as the elegant solution.

The vista that emerged was a tableau of dualities—the dance of particles and waves, the interplay of certainty and probability, the fusion of relativity and quantum mechanics. Classical physics, once the bedrock of knowledge, now stood as a stepping stone to the intricate realms of the quantum and the cosmic.

The transition wasn't seamless; it was marked by debates and philosophical ponderings. Albert Einstein's skepticism echoed through the corridors of discovery, questioning the compatibility of a universe governed by chance. Yet, amidst the debates and paradoxes, quantum mechanics stood firm, a testament to the limits of human intuition in a world of uncertainty.

Fields and quanta waltzed in a dance that promised to unveil the essence of reality. Yet, it wasn't without its challenges, as the intricacies of renormalization revealed the complex artistry of refining theories to mirror nature's subtleties.

And then, a name rose above the symphonic melody —a name that had been beckoning, a name that carried weight and promise. J. Robert Oppenheimer, with his brilliant mind and insatiable curiosity, entered the fray. His journey would encapsulate the spirit of an era—an era defined by relentless exploration, by pushing the boundaries of knowledge and imagination, and by wrestling with the mysteries of the universe, many of which he would provide answers to that are foundational to today's understanding of existence.

As the curtain fell on this prelude, a grand stage was set. The interplay of particles and fields, the dance of uncertainty and certainty, the quest for unification—all pointed to a future teeming with possibilities. And the next act, the story of J. Robert Oppenheimer's life and contributions were ready to unfold, carrying the torch of human curiosity and discovery into a new chapter of scientific history, one that would change science and politics forever.

Introduction

"Genius sees the answer before the question."
J. Robert Oppenheimer

In the pages of history, there are few whose lives serve to encapsulate the tumultuous evolution of human knowledge and the daunting ethical dilemmas that arise from one's own actions as much as Dr. Julius Robert Oppenheimer's, a man whose name is synonymous with brilliance and the unrelenting echoes of ethical dilemma.

Born on April 22nd, 1904, in the bustling heart of New York City, Oppenheimer's childhood was shaped by a strong emphasis on ethics and a clear appreciation for humanity. It was the cast that molded him into the world-renowned physicist and visionary who made every decision with a consideration for the ethical implications of his actions.

Oppenheimer made several staggering contributions to the fields of quantum mechanics and nuclear physics, significantly more than what most people know him for -- the atomic bomb, his contributions stretching from molecular physics to humanity's understanding of quantum singularities and black holes.

His life was wrought with personal and professional challenges, chief among them his frequent battles with depression, his struggle in the development of the atomic bomb, and his subsequent vilification by McCarthyism in the wake of the Second Red Scare.

A man whose very fiber was woven with ethics and humanity, he seemed to face divine irony when he was put in charge of the creation of a weapon that would be the single largest tool of mass destruction using the knowledge he had painstakingly acquired over a lifetime.

The story of the man who cast a shadow far larger than himself and in many ways continues to do so today, takes us on a journey of both intellect and emotion, duty and ethics, and even pain and joy. His tenure as director of the Los Alamos Laboratory was a race against time propelled by duty to his country, and a deep awareness of what would happen to the world if the Nazi regime acquired a working bomb first.

Oppenheimer was a pacifist by nature and had the added advantage of an astute intellect to see the reasoning against war, its atrocities, the destruction of life, and the shattering of families. But by all accounts, the war that the Nazis had waged needed to be stopped and the only way to do it was to harness the power of the atom before the Nazis did, providing the key motivation behind his efforts.

Part of a story that transcends just science, his work resulted in the closest humanity had ever come to an apocalyptic weapon, a power capable of destroying civilization as we know it. The soul shattering weight that bore down on Oppenheimer once the two bombs he created were dropped on Hiroshima and Nagasaki would remain until his untimely death in 1967.

That pain came to define much of his post-Manhattan Project life, and combined with his deep care for humanity, energized his campaign to curb the proliferation of atomic weapons and foster the peaceful application of nuclear technology. It pushed him to resist the terrible specter of high-yield strategic thermonuclear bombs, which, as weapons hundreds of times more devastating than the payloads dropped on Nagasaki and Hiroshima, continue to loom, ever-constant, like a grim shadow of death over our lives.

That shadow still remains for us now, as it did for him then.

Chapter 1 Family

"Those who say that the study of science makes a man an atheist, must be rather silly people."
Max Born

Born at the turn of the century into a wealthy family, Julius Robert Oppenheimer, or as he would come to be known affectionately to family and friends as J. Robert, was the older son of German-Jewish parents.

J. Robert's father, Julius Seliggman Oppenheimer, was born in the Hesse-Nassau province in the Kingdom of Prussia in May 1871, just four months after the unification of the German states into the German Empire.

Seventeen years later, in 1888, with antisemitism rearing its ugly head in Western and Central Europe, an impoverished and destitute Julius with no formal education of any kind left the Old World and sailed three thousand miles across the Atlantic to the shores of liberty, an utterly alien place to him where he did not even speak the language.

He spent the next two decades making his way up, and when Robert was born in 1904, he had managed to establish himself. He was now wealthy and was part of a major textile manufacturer in Manhattan, as well as an influential voice in the New York business world. In 1912, the year Robert's younger brother, Frank, was born, the Oppenheimers moved into a large apartment on

West 88th Street, overlooking the Central Park Reservoir.

Oppenheimer senior had realized the dream of the New World.

Housed in one of the richest neighborhoods in New York City at the time, their home hosted tasteful art, with walls adorned with Picassos, Van Goghs, and pieces of the avant-garde *Les Nebis* painter Édouard Vuillard.

Oppenheimer's youth was clearly a privileged one. Yet this did not make young Oppenheimer detached, owing largely to the great emphasis his parents placed on the importance of fairness, kindness, compassion, and ethics. Money and wealth were not about privilege in the Oppenheimer household. It was a means to do more for those who had less.

Oppenheimer's early years were marked by visits to Europe, particularly two of the world's great cultural centers, Paris and Berlin, which introduced him to the grandeur of art. This classical exposure was nurtured by his mother, and served to ignite within him a burning desire to explore the mysteries of the universe.

In art and culture, Oppenheimer also somehow saw the extent of human potential and caused him to seek out the true nature of who we are. It was not only the seeds that drew him to physics, it was the path that chartered his course to philosophy.

His mother, Ella Friedman, born on June 27th, 1869, in New York City was the daughter of Louis Friedman and Cecilia Eger. Ella Friedman was a gentle but gregarious soul whose artistic talent went beyond a casual relationship with art. She saw the world differently than others, and instilled that perspective into her son, J. Robert. She was a crucial element in her son's early development and was the source of his eventual fascination with the secrets of the universe.

This played a central role in molding Robert to become a unique kind of scientist who was focused on the mystical as well as the scientific, not rejecting something that wasn't purely tangible data, and as someone who saw the study of physics as something to run parallel to philosophy in the endeavor to unravel the secrets of existence.

She was also instrumental to the fostering of kindness and compassion within Oppenheimer that would prove to be core tenets of his character.

During a visit to a local park once, the young J. Robert witnessed a situation where an older child was teasing and excluding a younger child from playing with others. Ella intervened and spoke to the older child about kindness and fairness. This incident left a lasting impression on Oppenheimer, shaping his understanding of the importance of treating people with respect, compassion and dignity.

Though it wasn't just random events that little Oppenheimer witnessed. It was the kind of life his parents lived. During the holiday season, for instance, the Oppenheimer family would volunteer at a local shelter, serving meals to the homeless. The little boy observed his parents' dedication to helping others and witnessed how their actions aligned with the ethical values they often discussed at home.

As a child who exhibited a great and insatiable curiosity from an early age, his parents encouraged it, embracing his questions and guiding the discussions that followed. Ella taught him about history's great artists and thinkers, and his paternal grandfather introduced him to mineralogy. It was the first scientific field he was exposed to, and to which he quickly took a liking.

He became so fascinated with the subject that he became somewhat of an expert in it through reading and, in 1915, at just eleven years old, he was invited to give a lecture on the topic by the Mineralogical Club of New York City, whose members were surprised to learn he was just a skinny young boy. But he impressed them and was subsequently admitted to the society.

His curiosity and ability to learn quickly dovetailed nicely into the academic environment his parents placed him in. Young Oppenheimer was enrolled in the Ethical Culture Society School, one of New York City's best educational institutions.

This school, of which Oppenheimer's father, Julius, had been a member of the board of trustees for years by that point, had been founded in 1878 by the social ethics and political professor, religious leader, rationalist, social reformer and founder of the Ethical movement, Dr. Felix Adler. This movement, started in 1877 and which sought to provide a new ethical framework based on reason, compassion, and social responsibility, addressed issues such as morality and ethics while promoting social justice and advocating for the inherent worth and dignity of every human being.

Among many things, this led to the establishment of the Ethical Culture Society School, which was built upon those values and was designed to provide a holistic education that placed great emphasis on ethical values and social awareness.

Exemplified by its motto, "Deed, not creed," the school encouraged people to live according to their own principles, highlighting the importance of individual liberty and freedom, and to contribute positively to their communities, no matter their specific religious affiliations or beliefs.

Its commitment to social justice and advocacy for marginalized communities reflected its human-centered approach, and by actively addressing societal inequalities and promoting civil rights, its goal was to create a more equitable, just, and free society. It encouraged critical thinking, hands-on learning, and creativity. It fostered lively debate and discussion, creating an atmosphere of exploration framed by the emphasis on the inherent worth and dignity that every human being possesses, regardless of class, gender, race, origin, or creed.

While also being an example of academic excellence, the school evidently went beyond traditional academic subjects, focusing also on character development, social responsibility, and empathy. By integrating ethical principles into education, the school sought to produce graduates who were not only intellectually capable but also morally conscious and socially engaged.

Such was the environment in which young Oppenheimer developed, and such was the way that he would live his life, later becoming very politically active in the face of rising fascism in Europe. He would also become a member of the American Civil Liberties Union, for which he was later persecuted by the engine of McCarthyism, the FBI and Lewis Strauss during his 1953 security hearing, all of whom wrongly accused Oppenheimer of being a communist agent and who even branded the aforementioned civil rights organization as a "communist-front."

Oppenheimer's upbringing turned him into a compassionate and well-rounded individual who lived by the tenets of social responsibility and with great regard for the sanctity of human life and human rights. So deep was his care that we can only begin to imagine the great ethical and inner turmoil he experienced during the days of the Manhattan Project as he worked to design a weapon that was the most devastating the world had ever seen and would usher in an age where humanity teetered alarmingly on the brink of annihilation. Yet, Oppenheimer's concern for humanity also stands as a possible explanation for why he went through with the development of the bomb. In his mind, and in the minds of many others, from President Roosevelt to Major General Leslie Groves, who ran the project, and to the scientists who worked with him, there seemed to be a real chance that Nazi Germany was close to acquiring the technology to build such a weapon. The nightmarish specter of a nuclear Nazi regime and the devastation they would be able to wreak on the world with such a power convinced Oppenheimer that if someone had to have that power, it could not be the Nazis.

Even so, the atomic bombings of Japan, particularly the strike on Nagasaki, collectively killing over two hundred thousand civilians, not to mention the thousands more who died later from radiation poisoning, would crush his very soul and leave him in the dark and cold abyss of regret and depression for the rest of his life. All of this rings even more poignant when we recount Oppenheimer's words when he said his "life as a child did not prepare me for the fact that the world is full of cruel and bitter things."

He had developed a worldview that even his classmates at Harvard would describe as naive. So the tragedy of the Nazi and Imperial Japanese atrocities committed in the run-up to and during the Second World War doubtless fell on his shoulders harder than most, placing, in the folds of a sick joke, perhaps one of the most idealistic people in history in the position to develop the most devastating force ever unleashed on this earth.

But this was still decades to come, and in his youth, Oppenheimer displayed the stellar intellectual and academic abilities that would one day place him among history's most defining figures.

Chapter 2 Growing Up

"Science is not everything, but science is very beautiful."
J. Robert Oppenheimer

Already part of the Mineralogical Club at the tender age of eleven, Oppenheimer continued to demonstrate his growing academic prowess when he breezed through the third and fourth grades in just one year at Alcuin Preparatory School, another one of the New York City's finest, and was then fast-tracked through the eighth grade, completing his secondary school years at seventeen and graduating as valedictorian in 1921. His journey resembled a swift river, with intellectual currents pulling him towards deeper waters.

His scientific interest had also developed extensively by this point into the field of chemistry, which he would begin studying at Harvard after he enrolled in 1922.

Unfortunately, Oppenheimer contracted a nearly fatal case of dysentery during a family trip to Germany after his graduation from Alcuin, delaying his start at Harvard by a year. And after he spent months bedridden, his parents sent him to New Mexico to rest and recover in the scenic landscapes of the Land of Enchantment, hoping for him to regain his strength through outdoor experiences.

So for six weeks in the summer of 1922, he took up lodging in a so-called "dude ranch" twenty-five miles northeast of Santa Fe with his English high school teacher and mentor, Herbert Smith as his companion during this time. While there, Oppenheimer soaked in the beauty of the wide open West, and would go on five- or six-day trips through the countryside, including the Jemez Mountains and the hauntingly beautiful Sangre de Cristo Mountain Range with its snow-dusted peaks, towering pines and aspens that cast dappled shadows on the forest floor, and its crisp, pure air.

It was during one of these trips, when Oppenheimer ascended to the Pajarito Plateau, and made his way across the Valle Grande of the Valles Caldera, that he came up on the isolated Los Alamos Ranch School, whose location he would later choose as the site of the Los Alamos Laboratory, the center of the Manhattan Project.

After his convalescence was complete, Oppenheimer, now eighteen years of age, enrolled at Harvard College in September that same year, and began studying chemistry, before switching to physics. His wide array of scientific interests, beginning with mineralogy, helped mold him into someone who had a good grasp of multiple fields of science in a time when most were compartmentalized. It is ironic then, that for all Oppenheimer's genius in everything from molecular physics to the inner-workings of thermonuclear reactions, he was appallingly bad at arithmetic.

He began studying thermodynamics under the 1946 Nobel physics laureate Percy William Bridgman, whose research and experiments focused on the behavior of materials and substances under extremely high pressures. He developed techniques and equipment to study the properties of matter under these conditions, which led to significant advancements in our understanding of phase transitions, compression of materials, and the behavior of substances at extreme pressures.

He was a philosophical scientist who contemplated the foundations, reliability, and implications of science, and this no doubt had an effect on the young Oppenheimer who already placed great emphasis on the intangible as well as the tangible. Of his analytical nature, Oppenheimer said, "I found Bridgman a wonderful teacher because he never really was quite reconciled to things being the way they were and he always thought them out."

Following his emerging pattern first glimpsed at Alcuin, Oppenheimer blazed through his time at Harvard, reading voraciously and taking extra classes than was necessary, so that he completed his studies in just three years instead of four, graduating with a Bachelor of Arts *summa cum laude* in 1925. However, this meteoric success did not come without a great degree of stress, and while at Harvard he turned to smoking, a habit that would only grow throughout his life till he was smoking a hundred cigarettes per day.

A year earlier, in 1924, he was already accepted to Christ's College, Cambridge. Now, Oppenheimer wrote a letter to Ernest Rutherford, the pioneering physicist and 1908 Nobel chemistry laureate known as the father of nuclear physics for discovering nuclear half-life and its associated radiation, the one who theorized the existence of the neutron in 1920, and the then-head of the Cavendish Laboratory, for permission to work at the facility where such groundbreaking discoveries in the field of physics such as the discovery of protons and neutrons had been made.

Percy Bridgman had also written a letter of recommendation to his fellow scientist across the pond, and suggested that Oppenheimer was better suited to theoretical physics than the experimental, as he was a rather clumsy fellow.

Rutherford did not grant Oppenheimer his request, though it would be J.J. Thomson, who discovered the electron in 1897, who ultimately accepted him, provided that he undergo a basic laboratory course so that he would know his way around a lab and not cause any accidents.

Unfortunately, Oppenheimer found his time at Cambridge to be less than pleasant. As he said at one point, "I am having a pretty bad time. The lab work is a terrible bore, and I am so bad at it that it is impossible to feel that I am learning anything."

Owing partially to this, and substantially so to his growing interest in theoretical physics, not to mention the fact that Oppenheimer's trailblazing nature had caught the attention of Max Born future Nobel laureate Max Born, one of history's biggest contributors to the field of quantum physics, especially through his statistical interpretation of the wavefunction, Oppenheimer would leave Cambridge to study at the University of Göttingen in Germany to study under Born himself.

Life's intricate designs had already begun guiding Oppenheimer's fate in unexpected ways, as they would continue to do so for the rest of his life. And the invitation from Max Born, like a quill dipped in the inkpot of destiny, beckoned him to greater things. It was a catapulting launch in his academic pursuits that would bring him together with minds that would beat many paths to groundbreaking discoveries.

It was here that Oppenheimer truly thrived, far more than he ever did at Cambridge, and where he met and worked with many who would go on to become some of theoretical physics' greatest minds, several of whom would also later work with him on the Manhattan Project. Among them were Maria Goeppert Mayer, who won the Nobel Prize for proposing the nuclear shell model of atomic nuclei, Enrico Fermi, who, along with Leo Szilard, would build the world's first fully functional nuclear reactor, Edward Teller, the father of the hydrogen bomb, and Werner Heisenberg, Paul Dirac, Pascual Jordan, and Wolfgang Pauli.

Oppenheimer showed great enthusiasm in his studies at Göttingen, and lively debate and discussion was a common occurrence between him and his fellow students, even during class. But Oppenheimer had a habit of often taking over the whole conversation, so much so that his classmates drew up a petition to Professor Born threatening to boycott the class if he did not manage to get Oppenheimer to quiet down. Maria Goeppert, herself a signatory, presented it to the titan physicist, who did not address Robert directly about it, but rather left it out on his desk for the excited young man to see.

And so with not even a single word spoken, Oppenheimer quietened down.

Robert's time at Göttingen further reflected his academic precociousness when he completed his studies there in less than a year, attaining his PhD in physics in 1927 under Max Born's own supervision, at just twenty-three years old, years ahead of the average student. So sharp and adept was he that James Franck, the 1925 Nobel physics co-laureate with Gustav Hertz "for their discovery of the laws governing the impact of an electron upon an atom," who administered his oral exam, or *viva voce*, said he was glad when the examination was over, as Oppenheimer had seemed to be on the point of questioning him, so expertly and easily did he answer the questions.

Robert's formal education was essentially complete, but it was not just a stellar academic resume, what with his BA with *summa cum laude* honors from Harvard, stint at Christ's College, and PhD from Göttingen that he had to boast of. For, the same year he finished his studies, he co-authored and published a paper with Max Born called the Quantum Theory of Molecules, a seminal paper that introduced the Born-Oppenheimer Approximation.

This groundbreaking concept not only advanced the understanding of molecular dynamics but also bridged the gap between quantum chemistry and molecular physics, appropriately emerging in a time when the study of quantum mechanics was booming in Europe.

The paper delved into the fundamental behavior of molecules at the quantum level, providing a new framework to visualize and understand their intricate dynamics. Of central importance to this theory was the introduction of the Born-Oppenheimer Approximation.

The Approximation is a critical and defining concept in molecular physics that allows for the separation of nuclear and electronic motions within a molecule when considering molecular physics. It hinges on the idea that the nuclei within a molecule are significantly heavier than the electrons orbiting it. As a result, the nuclei are considered relatively stationary, acting as fixed points around which the lighter electrons move in a wave-like manner, resulting in dynamic movements influenced by their wave functions. With the already established Schrödinger equation for molecules to predict the movement of electrons, the Born-Oppenheimer Approximation simplified it by treating the electronic and nuclear motion independently, making it easier to study the movement of electrons without being distracted by that of nuclei.

The paper which remains Oppenheimer's most cited work, written when he was just twenty-three years old, and was a groundbreaking piece of academia in the field of molecular physics and quantum mechanics, Oppenheimer's detailed knowledge of both chemistry and physics were vital to the development of the Approximation, as quantum chemistry was a major element in the proof and supporting research.

Early Struggles

Unfortunately, Oppenheimer's life was not entirely a string of joy. In the tapestry of his accomplishments, and in the glow of his undeniable brilliance, there was, beneath the surface, a tempest of emotions and introspection. His journey was a mosaic of contrasts, from exuberant enthusiasm to introspective moments of sorrow. And amidst the triumphs, amidst the recognition and reputation he was building, he wrestled with his own demons, reminding us that even the stars that shine brightest carry weights and burdens like the rest of us.

To that end, he was, by this time, young as he was, already suffering from bouts of depression and emotional turmoil, also frequently finding himself battling anxiety. His classmates at Harvard and some of his teachers said that he portrayed some strange behavior, while others said he was an odd mix of intelligence and naivete, leading him to make bad decisions at times based on poor judgment and exaggerating a lot.

The exact root of Oppenheimer's depression is difficult to pinpoint, although it is likely that a factor was the treatment Oppenheimer faced as a Jew, both real and anticipated based on the presence alone of antisemitism, which had a darkening effect on his life.

But in the midst of all this, he could still be cheerful and sociable when he needed to be, although his default state was one of introversion.

He could also be profoundly arrogant, a trait that unfortunately caused many of his relationships to sour over time, but could also be generous intellectually, happy to speak to those who shared his passion for learning and who worked with him. And once he was friends with someone, he grew very close to them.

Oppenheimer also showed a great love for reading and the Greek and Latin classics of old, learning languages just to read texts in their original and unabridged form. He also had his first brush with Hinduism while at Harvard, a secular yet not solely secular interest that would turn into one of the most important pillars of his life.

Together with all of this, Oppenheimer was sometimes prone to fits of anger, as evidenced by the time he, according to his friend, Jeffries Wyman's account in the book *American Prometheus*, left an apple doused in an illness-inducing chemical on his professor Patrick Blackett's desk when he was at Cambridge, as a result of the tense relationship they had. Luckily, the future Nobel physics laureate did not eat the apple, but Oppenheimer was discovered and nearly expelled. It was his parents who convinced the university not to press charges and they subsequently arranged regular sessions for him with a psychiatrist on Harley Street in London.

In all this, we find, on a simplified level of course, that there were really three sides to Oppenheimer. The side which exhibited great intellectual and academic prowess, one which appeared unstable and erratic, but also one that was contemplative and inquisitive beyond the hard data that science provided. All of these parts of his constitution came together in a man who was both elusive and personable, distant yet greatly close to those he was friends with, and who, while adhering to the concrete and definitive nature of science, was open to the more ethereal perspectives of philosophy, as we will shortly see when, during his time as a professor at the University of California, Berkeley in the 1930s, he studied Sanskrit and read the *Bhagavad Gita*, one of Hinduism's most central documents which he ranked among the works that shaped his life.

Chapter 3 Star of Academia

"There is no place for dogma in science. The scientist is free, and must be free to ask any question, to doubt any assertion, to seek for any evidence, to correct any errors."
J. Robert Oppenheimer

After his time in Europe, Oppenheimer returned to the United States and spent the summer going on horse-packing trips with his younger brother, Frank, in New Mexico, much like he had done almost ten years earlier during his recovery from dysentery. During their time there, they leased a cabin in the Sangre de Cristo Mountains that Oppenheimer would eventually buy for $10,000 in 1947 and make his permanent home in later life, today the residence of his son, Peter Oppenheimer. In jest, he named it Perro Caliente, which is Spanish for "hot dog", for he had allegedly shouted that when he found out the cabin was available.

After his relatively brief vacation, considering the intense work he had just been consumed by during his time in Europe, Oppenheimer would return once again to the academic arena.

With his BA from Harvard and his PhD in physics from Göttingen and a groundbreaking contribution to science already under his belt, Oppenheimer's education was advanced further still when he was awarded a fellowship by the National Research Council. It furnished him with financial support and all the resources he needed to be able to focus solely on his academic pursuits. He spent a year of his fellowship at Harvard University in 1927, before going back across the pond under a fellowship from the International Education Board in 1928 to the University of Leiden in the Netherlands, where he got his nickname, Oppie, and the Eidgenössische Technische Hochschule, or ETH, in Zurich, the same research university Albert Einstein had attended in 1896. As yet another testament to Oppenheimer's unique academic ability and adeptness at learning, he learned the entire Dutch language in just 6 weeks to be able to give a technical talk in the country. A man with a feel for languages, for he preferred reading texts in their original writing, he now bordered on being a polyglot, as he spoke English, French, German, and Dutch with ease, not to mention Greek and Latin. He would later be one in full when he learned Sanskrit.

With his time at Leiden and Zurich complete, Oppenheimer's education was officially finished, though it can be said he would never stop learning, and he returned to the United States to begin a highly accomplished and noteworthy academic career that would span decades.

In 1929, at just twenty-five years old, he became an assistant professor of physics at the University of California, Berkeley. For over more than a decade between then and 1942, Oppenheimer would spend his time invigorating a new generation of scientists, teaching during the fall and winter semesters at Berkeley, and then at the California Institute of Technology, or Caltech, in the spring. His presence was an enigmatic dance between two prominent institutions, each representing a cornerstone of scientific education and exploration.

So, as the fall leaves painted the Berkeley campus with hues of gold and crimson, Oppenheimer donned his mantle of professorship. His lectures resonated through the echoing corridors. Eager students began to crowd his classroom not long after he began, drawn not only by the allure of his intellect but by his unique approach to teaching, for Oppenheimer's pedagogical methods were as groundbreaking as the scientific concepts he unraveled. He had a way of crafting narratives that illuminated the complexity of theoretical physics, making it accessible to those willing to dive into the intricate labyrinth of ideas.

When winter came, he went westward to Caltech. Spring's bloom was mirrored by the blossoming minds that attended his lectures. The university, renowned for its scientific prowess, had found a kindred spirit in Oppenheimer. Here, under the Southern Californian sun, he continued to sow the seeds of inspiration, the work he and his students would do leading to the establishment of California as a global scientific powerhouse. The United States had been largely silent in the realm of theoretical physics while Europe was advancing by leaps and bounds; Oppenheimer's work and those of his colleagues and students changed all of that and brought international attention.

The 1930s heralded a phase of recognition for Oppenheimer. His teaching methods had woven his name into the fabric of the American physics community. The corridors of academia were abuzz with tales of his captivating lectures. Students, hungry for enlightenment, flocked to his lectures at the School of Theoretical Physics that he himself had founded. It was here that the brightest minds of the era gathered, drawn like moths to the luminous flame of Oppenheimer's intellect.

As chalk met blackboard, equations flowed, and ideas swirled, Oppenheimer's influence rippling outward. He wasn't merely teaching the laws of physics; he was distilling the essence of scientific inquiry into the minds of the next generation. The legacy of his teaching methods was more than just intellectual nourishment; it was a torch passed on from one intellectual explorer to another.

Within the walls of Berkeley and the sprawling campus of Caltech, Oppenheimer's presence was more than a mere professorship – it was a gravitational force that shaped minds, ignited passions, and fostered an enduring love for the intricate tapestry of scientific exploration. He did not just teach his students the equations and numbers of science. He showed them its secrets, and how to get there. He showed them that as aspiring physicists, they were dealing with the most pressing questions facing humanity.

And so J. Robert Oppenheimer wove himself into the very fabric of academia, leaving an indelible mark that would echo through the corridors of knowledge for generations to come.

Amidst the scholarly fervor of the academic arena, a close-knit fellowship between him and a dozen of his brilliant students formed, and he would speak with them even outside school. Oppenheimer, the maestro of scientific inquiry, stood at the heart of their daily gatherings. With a demeanor that effortlessly combined intellectual rigor and charismatic ability, he orchestrated a symphony of minds. These dialogues were not mere academic formality; they were the crucible in which ideas were distilled and brilliance thrived.

Oppenheimer's probing questions acted as a beacon, guiding the scholars through the labyrinth of their own research pursuits.

His inquiries weren't meant to intimidate; they were an invitation to dig deeper, to explore uncharted territories of thought. With a sparkle in his eye and a warmth in his voice, he led these conversations down paths untraveled, encouraging his students to think beyond the obvious, to question assumptions, and to bridge the gaps between disciplines. The interactions were marked by a genuine exchange, where the boundary between teacher and student blurred, and the pursuit of knowledge became a collaborative venture.

They were best students, some of whom would go on to work with him, and were no ordinary scholars. They were handpicked advanced graduate students and seasoned research fellows, meticulously chosen to form a collective force of intellect under Oppenheimer's sagacious mentorship. This assembly of exceptional minds thrived within an environment where insatiable curiosity was the guiding star, and the language of inquiry flowed like an unbroken stream.

Among this select circle of inquisitive minds were individuals who would later etch their names in the pages of scientific history. From Richard Feynman, with his irrepressible curiosity and iconoclastic thinking, who revolutionized quantum electrodynamics and pioneered quantum computing, to Hans Bethe, known as the "Father of Nuclear Astrophysics," who deciphered the processes that power stars, and Murray Gell-Mann, a torchbearer of quantum chromodynamics who unraveled the inner workings of the atomic nucleus, theorizing quarks and leptons that reshaped the landscape of particle physics, illuminating a realm previously cloaked in obscurity.

Amidst the bustling laboratories and the fervent discussions that filled their days, a quiet corner was reserved for their shared love of learning. When they weren't discussing the secrets of the universe through the lens of physics, Oppenheimer and his colleagues sought refuge in the writings of Plato, delving into the philosopher's profound musings in their original Greek form, and he spent time of his own exploring further texts in Sanskrit and read the Bhagavad Gita. The lines on the pages seemed to bridge the gap between eras, connecting the present pursuit of knowledge with the philosophical inquiries that had stirred the minds of thinkers centuries before.

Amidst this kaleidoscope of intellectual curiosity, Oppenheimer's personal demeanor left an indelible mark on those around him. Hans Bethe painted a portrait of a man somewhat aloof from the currents of daily life when he recounted that while Oppenheimer grappled with the mysteries of particles and forces, the tremors of Wall Street's infamous Crash in 1929 reached his ears only months after the dust had settled. His engagement with the cosmos seemed to create a protective bubble around him, allowing him to traverse the realms of the profound while being temporarily shielded from the ripples of the mundane.

This might have made him seemingly detached from some things, but he was never negligent of the people around him, and his focus was all the more honed on the questions before him.

In the grand tapestry of scientific exploration, Oppenheimer's brilliance shone as a guiding star, illuminating paths to discovery that others dared not tread. One such journey began in the year 1930 when Oppenheimer, with the audacity of a true visionary, etched his name once again into the annals of scientific history. In a paper that seemed to dance at the edge of the known, he predicted the existence of the enigmatic positron, an antiparticle of the electron. Yet, like an intricate puzzle piece awaiting its perfect fit, this hypothesis yearned for confirmation.

It wasn't until 1932 that the puzzle found its missing fragment. Carl David Anderson, who worked with Oppenheimer at Caltech, unveiled the truth that had lurked within the shadows of theory. Anderson's meticulous experiments finally brought the positron to light, providing the undeniable evidence that completed Oppenheimer's prediction.

But the story doesn't end there, for Oppenheimer's thirst for knowledge was insatiable. He collaborated with Wendell Furry to breathe life into the electron-positron theory. Together, they refined this theory into a modern marvel, a composition of ideas that elegantly danced between the known and the mysterious. Their work wasn't confined to dusty journals or silent laboratories; it reverberated through the very fabric of the universe, unlocking secrets that had remained hidden until then.

As electrons and positrons engaged in a delicate cosmic ballet, Oppenheimer and Furry sought to comprehend the intricate steps of this mesmerizing dance. Their minds entwined and they painted equations that described not just the movements of these particles, but the essence of their interaction. It was a pursuit fueled by curiosity, a thirst for understanding that propelled them forward despite the intellectual challenges that lay in their path.

Oppenheimer, with his ever-curious mind, had shown the way, guiding the charge into uncharted territories where particles held secrets that defied simple explanations.

The Oppenheimer-Philips Process

At the same time, in the expansive realm of nuclear physics, where the invisible dance of subatomic particles orchestrates the secrets of matter, emerged yet another great duo that Oppenheimer was a part of, and whose collaboration would reverberate through the annals of scientific history.

Already recognized for his incisive intellect, Oppenheimer found an eager and exceptional partner in Melba Philips, a brilliant woman who shattered the glass ceilings of her time, making her mark in a scientific community that often seemed exclusionary. It would be yet another groundbreaking accomplishment for Oppenheimer, and only the first for his colleague, Melba Philips who, like him, was making waves very early on in her career. Standing as a symbol of triumph against the odds, she was a woman of remarkable intellect and tenacity, who navigated a scientific realm that often regarded her gender as a limitation. Her partnership with Oppenheimer was not just a collaboration of scientific minds; it was a testament to the indomitable spirit of those who dared to challenge the status quo.

Together, they embarked on an intellectual journey that would unveil the profound intricacies of atomic interactions.

And so it was that amidst the scientific fervor of 1935, a seminal idea was put forward—the Oppenheimer-Phillips Process. Born from the depths of their combined brilliance, this proposition illuminated the potential of a deuteron-induced nuclear reaction. A deuteron, composed of a neutron and a proton tightly bound in an atomic nucleus, harbored within it the power to instigate a transformative encounter with other nuclei.

The core of their proposal was elegantly simple yet conceptually profound. Picture the fusion of a neutron half of a deuteron with a nucleus, gracefully culminating in the expulsion of a proton. This mechanism, the cornerstone of the Oppenheimer-Phillips Process, could kindle a metamorphosis in elements, endowing them with radioactivity through the intervention of deuterons. Elements previously untouched by such transformations could be transformed.

What truly set this proposal ablaze was its revelation that nuclear interactions could transpire at energies far lower than previously imagined. The scientific landscape had hitherto assumed that these atomic liaisons required an energetic bombardment, akin to the celestial fury of cosmic rays. Yet, Oppenheimer and Philips illuminated an alternative path—a gentler, more nuanced approach where transformation emerged from a caress rather than a collision.

This discovery rippled through the scientific community, igniting a symphony of excitement and contemplation. The Oppenheimer-Phillips Process dismantled the barriers that confined nuclear interactions to the realm of high-energy extravaganzas. It reshaped the very understanding of how particles could engage in their intricate choreography, showing that even at lower energies, profound transformations could transpire.

In the tapestry of scientific breakthroughs, the significance of this collaboration was undeniable. It served as a testament to the power of human ingenuity, revealing that fresh perspectives could dismantle established notions. The Oppenheimer-Phillips Process extended an invitation to explore the nucleus with new eyes, to perceive its vulnerabilities and potentials in ways that once seemed beyond grasp.

In this narrative of intellectual kinship and groundbreaking revelation, Oppenheimer and Melba Philips emerged as pioneers of possibility. Their proposal resided not merely within the realm of equations and theories, but within the very fabric of how we understand the cosmos. As their idea spread, it breathed life into a new era of nuclear physics, one where the profound could emerge from the seemingly simple, where the dance of particles held the promise of unlocking the universe's most enigmatic secrets.

Chapter 4 Jean Tatlock

"I need physics more than friends."
J. Robert Oppenheimer

As we enter the next chapter of Oppenheimer's life, we also delve into the life of one of his most profound influences: Jean Tatlock. She went beyond being a mere acquaintance in Oppenheimer's story, helping to mold his intellectual perspective, to fan the flames of his philanthropic pursuits, and to leave an enduring imprint on his personal decisions.

Their relationship began casually in 1936 while Oppenheimer was teaching at Berkeley. The two were introduced by a mutual acquaintance and rapidly allowed their relationship to evolve into one which Oppenheimer elegantly summed up during his 1954 security hearing when he said, "We were at least twice close enough to marriage to think of ourselves as engaged."

Her involvement and dedication to the ethos of the Communist Party of the United States, or CPUSA, impacted every facet of her life and the lives of those close to her, ultimately casting a lengthy shadow over Oppenheimer's legacy. It is important to note, however, that her affinity to communism had no similarity to the Stalinist flavor of tyranny that communism had come to symbolize, and the baggage that word carried did not at all match her motivations, though that distinction would be completely lost on the engine of McCarthyism later on.

Tatlock's affinity to communist ideology was rooted in her desire to challenge established hierarchies and promote social justice—a commitment that resonated deeply with Oppenheimer. While he never formally joined the party, the couple's connection did showcase a profound meeting of hearts and minds over their shared empathy for humanity and the betterment of society. The principles of equitable distribution of resources and the empowerment of people aligned with their ideals and convictions.

Through her participation in the party, Tatlock demonstrated her readiness to engage in collective action against societal inequalities. She was highly aware of the struggles of the people and believed that communism was the only way to address it.

Her alignment with the Communist Party also mirrored the prevailing political climate of her time, a period marked by intense discussions about communism's potential implications, both infused with fervor and shadowed by controversy. This era witnessed the ominous ascent of European fascism, a looming evil that often seemed to leave communism as the only way to respond to it.

Amidst all this, it's crucial to underscore that Tatlock's political involvement was just one thread within the intricate tapestry of her multifaceted life. Beyond her political convictions, her intellectual pursuits, personal struggles, and her sway over figures like Oppenheimer enriched her narrative, her legacy transcended the role of a mere footnote in Oppenheimer's life.

Born into the generation deeply affected by the Great Depression, Tatlock's life journey was indelibly shaped by the harsh realities she witnessed. She was just 15 when the effects of the Great Depression hit the nation. The widespread suffering and agony she encountered evoked a logical psychological response: the earnest desire to alleviate the pain endured by those in distress. This innate motivation formed the bedrock of her embrace of communist ideals.

She boasted an illustrious educational journey spanning Vassar College and Stanford Medical School where she studied psychiatry, her pursuits underscoring her profound fascination with untangling the intricate complexities of human cognition and behavior. This advanced academic background endowed her with the intellectual acumen necessary to recognize and comprehend the injustices afflicting a significant portion of society.

Her academic voyage not only showcased her dedication but also hinted at her intrinsic curiosity about the inner workings of individuals. However, her inquisitiveness extended beyond the confines of her chosen field. Tatlock's familial backdrop added another layer of depth to her persona. Her father, John Strong Tatlock, was no ordinary figure – he was a renowned scholar celebrated for his mastery of Geoffrey Chaucer and Middle English literature. Growing up in an environment steeped in scholarly exploration, it's conceivable that Jean's own intellectual inclinations were influenced by her father's legacy. The roots of her scholarly pursuits might have intertwined with her family's literary affinities, fostering a multidimensional approach to her academic pursuits.

Through her education and upbringing, Tatlock's journey became a tapestry woven with threads of psychiatry, literature, and familial intellectualism. These facets of her life would later intertwine with her connection to J. Robert Oppenheimer, forming a unique bond founded on shared interests and a quest for intellectual exploration. The unfolding narrative of her life would reveal not only her academic prowess but also her ability to foster connections that transcended the boundaries of conventional relationships.

Tatlock's and Oppenheimer's was a nuanced journey that ebbed and flowed, much like the tides of intellectual exploration. Their connection wasn't a continuous, unbroken line, but rather a series of on-and-off episodes that shaped their interactions, defined by the intellectual exploration they were both fascinated by.

Their relationship was marked by periods of closeness and moments of distance. At times, their exchanges were frequent and intense, with their shared interests in literature and the world of ideas acting as magnetic forces that drew them together, while at others the currents of life carried them apart. Responsibilities, academic pursuits, and personal endeavors sometimes created gaps in their interactions. During these times, their connection dimmed and their dialogues turned to a whisper, but they would always renew with the same intellectual flames, until they didn't in 1939.

This ebb and flow wasn't a sign of instability; instead, it showcased the depth and authenticity of their relationship. Their ability to reconnect and reignite their discussions demonstrated the enduring nature of their intellectual camaraderie.

In understanding their relationship's rhythm, we glimpse the authenticity of their connection. It wasn't a fairy tale with a linear plot; instead, it was a dynamic narrative woven with threads of shared passions, individual growth, and the intricate dance of their intellectual explorations.

The surviving letters and correspondence between Tatlock and Oppenheimer offer a precious glimpse into the tapestry of their unique relationship.

These written conversations weren't mere pleasantries; they were explorations.

Their correspondence also speaks to the profound influence they had on each other and their perspectives. Tatlock's insights served as prisms that refracted new shades of understanding for Oppenheimer on subjects that varied from life to politics. In turn, his insight expanded her horizons into the world of science and philosophy, offering fresh angles through which she could view the world. This interplay of ideas was a testament to the richness of their connection – a connection that thrived not just in physical proximity but also in the realm of written words.

Through their discussions, she fanned the flames of his interest in the events of the world – the Spanish Civil War, the rise of fascism in Nazi Germany and Italy, pressing matters that shaped the course of history.

His decision to vote for the first time in the 1936 US presidential election and his commitment to allocate a portion of his annual salary – a substantial 3% – to support Jews fleeing Europe during the tumultuous years leading up to World War II was a profound reflection of Oppenheimer's convictions, put to good use with the awareness of world affairs he gained as he watched the disturbing rise of the Nazis. This philanthropic dedication wasn't born in isolation; it bore the fingerprints of his conversations with Tatlock, not to mention his upbringing. Through their discussions on societal matters, political upheavals, and the rise of fascism, she had ignited a spark that resonated deeply within Oppenheimer, which coupled with his humanist values, propelled him to take action against darkness.

The relationship between Tatlock and Oppenheimer was a dynamic one that reverberated not only in their personal lives but unfortunately also within the broader context of political scrutiny. Their connection was marked by its own rhythm of closeness and distance, but its echoes carried far beyond their conversations. As Oppenheimer navigated the tumultuous waters of his 1954 security hearing, spurred on by the hysteria of McCarthyism that gripped the nation at the time, the specter of Tatlock's Communist Party affiliation and his affiliation with her was used against him to question his loyalty and honor, and cited as evidence of his potential sympathies towards ideologies considered antithetical to American values. In the courtroom, the nuances of their intellectual exchanges and the depth of their connection were overshadowed by the political implications of her beliefs.

Tatlock's life was an intricate tapestry woven with threads of brilliance, struggle, and heartache. Within the narrative of her academic pursuits, her profound connection with Oppenheimer, and her unyielding commitment to political causes, there lay a haunting undercurrent of personal battles that ultimately led to a tragic and heart-wrenching end.

While her intellectual pursuits illuminated her mind and her engagement in political discourse ignited her passion, Tatlock grappled with a formidable adversary – clinical depression. Despite her outward achievements and her ability to engage with the world's complexities, the weight of this internal battle cast a perpetual shadow over her thoughts. The juxtaposition of her intellectual prowess with the darkness within serves as a poignant reminder that even the brightest minds can be clouded by the burden of mental anguish.

Yet, Tatlock's struggles were not limited to the realm of depression alone. Within the societal norms of her time, her internal conflict regarding her sexual orientation added layers of complexity to her inner turmoil. The condemnation and lack of understanding surrounding homosexuality compounded her distress, creating a whirlpool of confusion and self-doubt. It's a painful testament to the societal pressures that can exacerbate the inner struggles individuals face, as they grapple with their identities in a world that often fails to provide acceptance and empathy, and basic recognition of their humanity.

Amidst these storms of emotion, the trajectory of Tatlock's life took a tragic turn. On January 4th, 1944, the weight of her personal battles became unbearable, and she made the heartbreaking decision to end her own life. The brilliance that had once illuminated her thoughts and the fervor that had fueled her commitment to change were tragically overshadowed by the darkness she fought within herself.

Tatlock's story serves as a poignant reminder of human fragility. Her journey is a testament to the complexity of brilliance, the depth of personal struggles, and the often unspoken battles that individuals wage within their hearts and minds. In a world that often celebrates achievements while shunning vulnerability, her narrative calls for a compassionate acknowledgment of the complexities that lie beneath the surface.

Her life also underscores the critical importance of mental health support and understanding, as well as the urgent need for societies to evolve beyond judgment and embrace the diversity of human experiences, including our choice of who we love. It's a stark reminder that the weight of societal expectations and the lack of acceptance can amplify personal struggles, highlighting the need for a more inclusive and empathetic world.

In commemorating Tatlock's life, we honor not only her intellect and her commitment to change but also the struggle she endured in navigating the complexity of her own emotions. Her legacy is a call to recognize the humanity that resides within every individual – a reminder that compassion, understanding, and support can make a profound difference in the lives of those who silently fight the pain roiling within them.

As for Oppenheimer, the news of Tatlock's tragic fate saddened him deeply, despite them no longer being together and him being already married to the botanist and chemist Katherine Oppenheimer.

Mary Ellen Washburn, Jean's landlady, had called Charlotte Serber, a journalist, statistician and the Manhattan Project's librarian, as well as the wife of physicist Robert Serber, who worked on the project with Oppenheimer, to tell her what had happened. Charlotte informed her husband, who carried the news to Oppenheimer's office, but when he got there, Oppenheimer was already aware. It turned out that Tatlock's phone had been tapped by the FBI, and so J. Edgar Hoover was one of the first people to know of her passing, and Army Intelligence informed Captain Peer de Silva, the Laboratory's security chief, who then told Oppenheimer.

In tribute to her, as she had introduced him to the poetry of John Donne, he would name the first atomic weapons test in history "Trinity," in reference to one of his works.

"I did suggest it... Why I chose the name is not clear," Oppenheimer later wrote in a reply to his friend Leslie Groves who had asked him about the origins of the name, "but I know what thoughts were in my mind. There is a poem by John Donne, written just before his death, which I know and love.

"From it, a quotation:

As West and East

In all flat Maps—and I am one—are one,

So death doth touch the Resurrection."

Chapter 5 Katherine Oppenheimer

The woman who would become Oppenheimer's one and only wife of nearly three decades and the mother of his children, Peter and Katherine, her life was a chaotic thrill of political intrigue, intellectual exploration, and romantic storms before they met in the summer of 1939.

Born on August 8, 1910, in Recklinghausen, Germany, as Katherine Vissering Puening, or Kitty, as she was affectionately known by friends and family, she was the only child of Franz Puening and Käthe Vissering. When she was three years old, her father was hired by a steel company in Pittsburgh after his invention of a new kind of blast furnace, and so the family set sail for a new life in the United States, anchoring themselves in the suburb of Aspinwall, Pennsylvania, just outside Pittsburgh. Though she did not speak English at the time, she mastered the language very easily and would go on to speak both English and German fluently without any accent.

The rest of her childhood was punctuated with frequent summer trips to Germany, and fifteen years later, she graduated Aspinwall High School in 1928, after which she enrolled at the University of Pittsburgh, where her thirst for knowledge led her to subjects like mathematics, biology, and chemistry.

Two years later, in March of 1930, she went on a transformative sojourn to Europe which would result in her meeting her first husband, Frank Ramseyer, an American music student who was studying in Paris. She returned only two months later on May 19th, and completed the first year of her degree, before marrying Ramseyer before a Justice of the Peace on December 24th, 1932, after which they moved into an apartment near Harvard University, where her newly-wed husband hoped to achieve a degree in music.

For her part, she re-enrolled at the University of Pittsburgh the January of the following year, but would eventually transfer to the University of Wisconsin in June, after a trip across the Atlantic again with Ramseyer. Finally, on December 20th, 1933, three days short of one year since they were married, Katherine had their marriage annulled by the Superior Court of Wisconsin, owing to turmoil during their marriage and her discovery of his drug addiction.

Not long after, at a New Year's Eve party, Puening would come face to face with Joseph Dallet Jr., a former steel worker turned union organizer, who had joined the Communist Party of America in 1929, and had been part of the International Unemployment Day protest in Chicago resulting from the joblessness crisis of the era and which was brutally repressed by the authorities.

A few months later, with her father Franz representing a Chicago-based company, her parents moved to Claygate near London. And after visiting her family in Europe, Puening returned to the United States on August 3rd, 1934, and moved in with Dallet into a run down boarding house which cost them $5 a month, just down the hall from future political giants Gus Hall and John Gates, the latter especially known for his attempt to liberalize the American Communist Party and lessen the restrictions it advocated for. They lived on the dole, receiving $12.50 per month each.

Puening was allowed to join the Communist Party, as she was the common-law wife of a member, but she had to first prove her loyalty by distributing *Daily Worker* copies on the streets. Her party dues were 10c a week.

It was thus during her unofficial marriage to Dallet and the connections that followed from it that Puening was introduced to the world of politics, which lead to her ultimately being a staunch member of the party, whose values, it must be said again, were and are the extreme opposite of the twisted authoritarian scourge of Stalin and the Soviet Union.

She and Dallet separated for a while in June 1936, after which she moved to London and worked as a German-to-English translator. For months, she did not receive a single letter from Dallet, but it wasn't long after that that she discovered her mother had been hiding the letters he sent. Her mother was a "very repressive woman," as her friend, Anne Wilson said.

The last of these letters from Dallet that her mother had hidden told her that he was departing for Spain aboard the RMS *Queen Mary* to join the International Brigades, of whom there were volunteers from all over the world, including America, fighting in the Spanish Civil War against Franco's fascist forces.

She subsequently went to Cherbourg, in France, where she met up with Dallet and his best friend Steve Nelson. They went to Paris together, and after a few days, she went back north to London while Dallet turned south towards Spain, where he joined the Mackenzie-Papineau Battalion, a unit of American and Canadian volunteers.

Puening wanted to join him in Spain, and she was able to secure permission. Unfortunately, she was unable to do so as she had to undergo an operation on August 26th, 1937 for what was at first thought to be appendicitis, but was actually ovarian cysts. With the procedure complete, she was forced to stay in Britain to recover. Sadly, she would never join Dallet, for while she was recuperating she received word that he had been killed in action on October 17th, 1937. The letters he wrote to her were later compiled and published in 1938 *Letters from Spain by Joe Dallet, American Volunteer, to his Wife*.

Though they had been together for only two years and spent several months separated, Dallet had left a lasting impression on Puening, awakening her political interests and her care for social change and progress. Dallet was to Puening what Tatlock was to Oppenheimer. Dallet, like Tatlock, was the politically active one in the relationship, and introduced his partner to pressing concerns in society and inspired her own drive to make a difference. And the values that Katherine built on as a result of her relationship with Dallet were ones that Oppenheimer was building on at the time as well, and theirs would eventually merge and amplify like constructive interference experienced when the highest points of two waves overlap, resulting in an even bigger one.

Later, Puening went to see Nelson in Paris, who was recovering from a wound he had sustained in August, and together they went back to the United States where she lived for two months with Nelson and his wife in Brooklyn. After that, she went back to the Keystone State to see her friend Zelma Baker at the Cancer Research Institute of the University of Pennsylvania, where she enrolled.

It was here that she met Richard Stewart Harrison, an Oxford medicine graduate who was finishing his internship. They got married on November 23rd, 1938, after which she left the Communist Party.

Shortly afterward, Richard left for Pasadena to begin his medical residency at the California Institute of Technology, while Katherine, whose last name was now Harrison, stayed in Philadelphia, diligently completing her studies in botany at the University of Pennsylvania. Her academic achievements opened doors, securing her a prestigious postgraduate research fellowship at the University of California, Los Angeles.

There, she collaborated with physicist Charles Lauritsen, working in laboratories that echoed with the resonance of both physics research and experimental cancer therapy. Kitty's intellectual curiosity had found its home. And it was amidst this environment that an intriguing crossroads emerged. A garden soiree orchestrated by Lauritsen and his wife Sigrid in August 1939 brought Kitty face to face with a rising star in the scientific world whose light was only growing brighter, J. Robert Oppenheimer. This meeting set in motion a remarkable transformation of her life's trajectory.

The magnetic pull between them was immediate and undeniable. So their connection ignited, and they spent a great deal of time together, symbolized at first by the drives they went on with each other.

During one festive holiday season, Kitty embarked on a solitary journey to Berkeley, seeking the company of Oppenheimer. This juncture marked a transformation beyond the conventional, the depth of their commitment hinted at in shared moments against the backdrop of Berkeley's charm.

Oppenheimer later invited Katherine and Richard to his ranch in New Mexico. Richard's professional commitments did not allow him to accept, but Kitty seized the opportunity with eagerness. With Robert Serber and his wife Charlotte, Kitty arrived at Perro

Caliente where she met up with J. Robert and his brother Frank, and his wife, Jackie.

Here, the picturesque Sangre de Cristo Mountains bore witness to their shared experiences and the horsepacking trips she went on together with the Oppenheimers.

Kitty, already certain Oppenheimer was the man she wanted to spend the rest of her life with, orchestrated their marriage through pregnancy, as she told her friend, Anne.

After she was pregnant, Kitty told Oppenheimer, after which, in September 1940, he told Harrison the news. A collective decision formed, mapping out a journey where Kitty's divorce would pave the way for her union with J. Robert. Shortly afterward, amidst a platform for Spanish Civil War refugees, Robert stood to proclaim his engagement to Kitty, an announcement tinged with a touch of sentiment as Nelson's family was also expecting, whom they named Josie in honor of their friend Joseph Dallet, Jr.

The proceedings of Kitty's and Richard's divorce unfolded, with her moving to Reno, Nevada for six weeks to meet the state's residency criteria, after which, on November 1, 1940, the final strokes were added to her divorce, setting the stage for a swift and momentous event. The dawn of November 2, 1940, witnessed a modest civil ceremony in Virginia City, Nevada, where Katherine Puening and J. Robert Oppenheimer intertwined their destinies. This union stood as a transformative milestone in their lives, an amalgamation of two trajectories guided by twists of fate, intellectual endeavors, and shared experiences. And the stage was set for Katherine Oppenheimer to become a central figure in the life of one of history's most distinguished scientists.

Chapter 6 Manhattan Project

"People who talk of outlawing the atomic bomb are mistaken
- what needs to be outlawed is war."
Major General Leslie Groves

It was August, 1942 and Europe lay in ruins. Its people languished under the cruel and inhuman grasp of the Nazi war machine. Hitler's regime of terror, like an insatiable leviathan, had swallowed nations whole, leaving in its wake a trail of desperation, death, and despair.

Standing up to this evil was a moral necessity.

From the shores of the English Channel to the frigid waters of the Baltic and North Seas, from the windswept plains of Eastern Europe and soon even to the deserts of North Africa, the swastika fluttered ominously, casting a dark and demonic shadow over war-torn lands.

This was not a war as usual. This was something different. It wasn't just two sides fighting over land and resources. It was a moral war. The Nazi machinery of terror was fueled by hatred and bigotry. Their goal was not limited to exploiting the land and sacking the resources. They wanted entire swathes of people killed because they looked different, or spoke differently.

Even by this point in the war the Nazis were not yet at the height of their expansion. The Nazi war effort was only ramping up, and found conventional weapons could be improved upon. For three years now, the regime had been exploring the idea of harnessing the power of the atom to build a nuclear bomb.

Known in Germany as *Uranprojekt,* or Uranium Project, the program had started just months after the discovery of nuclear fission in 1938 by the physicists Lise Meitner and Otto Robert Frisch, together with chemists Otto Hahn and Fritz Strassman.

Fortunately for the rest of the world, the program quickly ran into trouble and was put on hold because many of Germany's prominent physicists had been drafted into the armed forces. It was on September 1st, 1939, the day Nazi Germany unleashed its evil in the invasion of Poland, sending over a million men and thousands of tanks and planes storming across the border that the German Army Weapons Agency restarted the program.

For the next six years, until the capture of Germany's nuclear research facilities by Allied forces in 1945, the Nazis worked to achieve nuclear energy and weapons, attempting to build reactors as well as bombs.

However, thanks to the persistent shortage of physicists, partly due to the Nazi purges of Jewish scientists, as well as the brave resistance of the Norwegian people who kept heavy water, a crucial component in the process, the German nuclear program was sufficiently impeded.

Fate, it seems, had conspired with the Allies and denied Hitler his nuclear weapon.

The Allies, however, weren't the wiser. They believed, by all credible intelligence, that Germany was moving full steam ahead with their nuclear ambitions.

For the Nazis, a genocidal and inhuman regime that was committing the greatest atrocities humanity had ever been cursed to witness, to wield such an apocalyptic power was beyond imagination, and unacceptable. Appeasement and moral objection to war was not an option.

***

The path to the atomic bomb began on August 2nd, 1939, one month after the start of the war in Europe. Physicist and refugee Leo Szilard, who had fled fascist Italy not long before, penned a letter to President Roosevelt warning of the possibility of a catastrophic device that was the natural progression from gaining the knowledge of nuclear fission. Szilard was convinced the Nazis would attempt to build it.

But the process was not without its challenges.

Szilard, fearing his name did not carry enough weight, needed someone of universal recognition to vouch for his message. So he turned to Albert Einstein who was, by this point, teaching at Princeton University and well aware of the lengths the Nazis would go to for world domination.

Fueled by a sense of dire urgency, Szilard got his friend, Edward Teller, to drive him to Einstein's summer house on Long Island and presented his letter to Einstein personally.

It did not take long for Einstein to add his signature, for he too understood the chilling prospect of a Nazi nuclear weapon. As Teller said, he "read it, asked a few questions about it, and then said, yes, yes, and signed it."

In their letter, Szilard and Einstein outlined the startling potential of nuclear fission – the process that could release an immense amount of energy through splitting atomic nuclei. Known as the Szilard-Einstein letter, it was a desperate plea to bring to light the immense danger posed by the Nazi regime's nuclear experiments.

Their concern was well-founded, as Germany had already accumulated a roster of brilliant scientists who were making strides in nuclear research. The letter's urgency stemmed from the realization that Nazi Germany might harness this scientific breakthrough to build a weapon of unprecedented destruction.

However, the impact of the letter was not immediate. It took some time for the significance of the Szilard-Einstein letter to be fully comprehended. Once President Roosevelt realized the weight of the situation, he established the Advisory Committee on Uranium in October 1939. This committee, led by the physicist Lyman J. Briggs, was tasked with evaluating the potential of nuclear fission for military purposes and advising the government on the matter.

The road ahead was not without its challenges. The endeavor was shrouded in secrecy, and absolute secrecy is in itself an impediment to progress. The stakes were high. The brightest minds in the scientific community were enlisted and their expertise harnessed to unlock the secrets of nuclear fission. As laboratories hummed with activity, the drive to understand the underlying science behind nuclear reactions intensified.

Then came December 7th, 1941 and Japan attacked Pearl Harbor. This forced America's hand to fully immerse it in the global conflict. Facing the Axes of Evil, coupled with the pressing awareness of Nazi nuclear ambitions and the recommendations of the Advisory Committee on Uranium, spurred the American government to allocate significant resources to the then-nascent nuclear research effort.

Prompted by this confluence of events, in the fall of 1942, President Franklin D. Roosevelt ordered the start of the Manhattan Project in a race against time. It electrified the scientific community and propelled the United States into a frenzied quest for the most potent weapon the world had ever seen.

Major General Leslie Groves, the Army Corps of Engineers officer who had built the Pentagon, was appointed director of the Manhattan Project. Among his duties, he had to hire the director of the Los Alamos Laboratory. The director would be the key person in directing and bringing America's nuclear ambition to fruition. Groves began his tenure with the objective of securing a Nobel Prize-winning physicist for the post. He wanted someone with academic gravitas to lead the formidable assembly of scientific minds.

However, after interviewing Oppenheimer, Groves realized that no stack of academic qualifications could not encapsulate the depth of intellect and innate leadership skills that Oppenheimer possessed. Oppenheimer's uncanny ability to grasp the crux of any subject, coupled with his tenacity and hands-on approach, made him a natural choice.

Groves chose him without any reservation.

***

Now appointed as the head of the project to develop the first nuclear weapon, it was up to Oppenheimer to select a location for the work to take place. It had to be remote and isolated. Security and secrecy was paramount, but Oppenheimer also knew that the final product needed to be tested and the fallout could not be in an area that was populated.

He chose a site in New Mexico near the Valle Grande of the Valles Caldera where he had traveled with his brother in the late 1920s. It was in the desert, thirty-five miles from Santa Fe and surrounded by nothing but sand, in what would later become Los Alamos County in 1949. The only inhabitants in the vicinity were the residents of the McDonald Ranch, whom the US Army vacated from the site prior to construction.

Construction on the top secret compound began almost immediately, during which Oppenheimer worked out of the Manhattan Project's office on 270 Broadway, in Manhattan.

The building still stands today.

Oppenheimer had not initially realized the sheer number of people who would be working under him at the Los Alamos Laboratory. At the height of its activity, five thousand people called Los Alamos home.

But even with the size of the Los Alamos Laboratory and the work that was done there, it was, while central, by far not the only piece in the puzzle. The entire Manhattan Project employed, all in all, about 130,000 people. This included Enrico Fermi and Leo Szilard's work in Chicago which produced the world's first nuclear reactor, the uranium enrichment sites in Oak Ridge, Tennessee, and the Hanford Site in Washington.

First Nuclear Reactor

In the pages of scientific history, few feats loom as large as the creation of the first working nuclear reactor. This pioneering endeavor, undertaken by the brilliant minds of Enrico Fermi and Leo Szilard, marks a pivotal moment in the trajectory of human discovery and innovation.

Their journey to harness the power of the atom, culminating in the construction of the Chicago Pile-1 reactor, not only reshaped the scientific landscape but also sent ripples across the geopolitical fabric of the 20th century. Their work, as part of the Manhattan Project eventually, was a building block of Oppenheimer's work at Los Alamos.

Fermi, who was hailed as "the Pope of Physics," possessed a sharp, methodical mind. His pioneering work in quantum mechanics had earned him international acclaim, and his adeptness with mathematical abstraction was matched only by his practicality in experimentation.

Leo Szilard, on the other hand, was a physicist of immense creativity and foresight. A prodigious thinker, he had envisioned the concept of the nuclear chain reaction – a cascade of atom-splitting events that could release an extraordinary amount of energy.

Since the discovery of fission in 1938, Szilard was all but certain about its potential, and hypothesized that a self-sustaining nuclear chain reaction could be achieved, leading to an outpouring of energy with untold applications. Yet, this idea was not without its challenges. The theoretical groundwork was complex, and the practical hurdles immense.

As Szilard's thoughts on nuclear chain reactions took shape, he sought a collaborator who could bridge the gap between theory and practice. This search led him to Enrico Fermi, whose formidable analytical prowess and knack for experimentation seemed tailor-made for the endeavor. And between Szilard's theoretical brilliance and Fermi's practical finesse, the partnership blossomed.

The duo embarked on a journey to decipher the intricate relationship between atoms. They generated reams of calculations and equations that navigated the yet unknown path to a controlled nuclear chain reaction as they grappled with the enigma of critical mass – the precise amount of fissile material needed to initiate a self-sustaining reaction. It was a puzzle that required not just theoretical ingenuity, but empirical validation.

Their calculations led to a groundbreaking realization: a self-sustaining chain reaction was theoretically possible, but it required a delicate balance.

As they delved into their research, Fermi and Szilard found that their theoretical journey extended beyond nuclear reactions to encompass the fundamental physics of neutrons and their role in the process. They realized that the key to controlling a nuclear chain reaction lay in the moderation of neutrons to slow them down, increasing the chances of their successful interaction with fissile nuclei.

This was a key breakthrough.

The pair's theoretical insights were crucial not only for conceptualizing the reactor but also for guiding the subsequent experimental design. Before long, they found that carbon, in graphite form, could serve as a suitable moderator to slow down the neutrons. This insight would prove invaluable in the construction of the first nuclear reactor.

Fermi, for his part, was exceptionally skilled at translating complex theoretical concepts into practical calculations. His rigorous approach ensured that their theories were not just abstract concepts but could be applied to the real world. This skill in bridging theory and application would become a hallmark of Fermi's approach to nuclear science.

But even as they refined their theories, Fermi and Szilard grappled with the ethical implications of their work. They were acutely aware of the dual potential of nuclear fission—both as a means to harness energy for humanity's benefit and as a source of unprecedented destruction. Their conversations extended beyond the technicalities of their research to discussions about the responsible use of their discoveries.

In 1942, as construction of the experimental reactor, Chicago Pile-1, began, Fermi's and Szilard's theories were put to the ultimate test and forever alter the course of human history.

Building Chicago Pile-1

The undertaking to construct the world's first nuclear reactor was nothing short of audacious, with the results of the experiment determining the fate of the entire Manhattan Project.

The University of Chicago's football stadium, Stagg Field, was chosen as the site for this groundbreaking experiment. A network of graphite blocks, uranium pellets, and cadmium control rods were meticulously assembled within a makeshift "pile" structure, all aimed at achieving the delicate balance required for a controlled chain reaction.

The shortage of materials during wartime imposed further challenges. Uranium metal, in particular, was in short supply, leading to the use of uranium oxide. But the challenges didn't end there—finding a suitable neutron source and ensuring the safety of the team were paramount concerns.

Finally, as December 2, 1942 dawned over the University of Chicago's Stagg Field, a sense of anticipation and trepidation hung heavy in the air. Fermi, methodical and composed as ever, gradually pulled control rods from the pile, allowing neutrons to infiltrate the uranium nuclei.

It was noon.

Minutes stretched into hours as the scientists monitored the instruments, waiting for the telltale signs of a self-sustaining chain reaction. Then, a faint but unmistakable signal was recorded—a steady increase in the neutron count indicated that Chicago Pile-1 was achieving criticality--a controlled nuclear chain reaction was underway.

In a characteristic display of understatement, Fermi turned to his colleague Herbert L. Anderson and remarked, "The Italian navigator has just landed in the new world." It was a reference to Columbus' discovery of America, highlighting the significance of their achievement as a groundbreaking exploration into the realm of nuclear science.

The success of Chicago Pile-1 not only validated the theories and calculations of Fermi and Szilard but also set the stage for subsequent developments in the

Manhattan Project. The experiment had profound implications for both peaceful and military applications of nuclear technology, with consequences that continue to shape global politics and scientific endeavors to this day.

The immediate aftermath of the Chicago Pile-1's success reverberated through the scientific community, and had confirmed the theoretical basis for building an atomic bomb. But, it was already clear that nuclear power had another outlet - energy. The controlled chain reaction demonstrated the feasibility of such power, offering a clean and nearly limitless source of energy. This realization would drive further research into peaceful applications of nuclear technology, a cause President Eisenhower would later seriously undertake, eventually leading to the development of commercial nuclear reactors for electricity generation.

Still, Fermi and Szilard knew what their work was giving way to, and they would later take steps to try and mitigate the wrath of the atomic bomb. They, along with other scientists, drafted the "Szilard Petition" in 1945, urging the US government to avoid using the bomb on Japan without warning and to promote international cooperation on nuclear technology. Although their plea was not heeded, the petition foreshadowed the later efforts to establish arms control treaties.

It's no question the ethical dilemmas that loomed over the project, and no wonder then that Fermi, ever the cautious physicist, reportedly had sleepless nights before the reactor's first test. He understood that science could no longer remain in the realm of abstract equations; but had the power to reshape the world in profound ways. The questions of responsibility and ethical considerations surrounding scientific discovery had become unavoidable.

In the years following the success of Chicago Pile-1, both Fermi and Szilard continued to contribute significantly to the scientific community and to societal discussions about nuclear technology. Szilard, for one, remained an advocate for arms control, dedicating his later years to global efforts to limit nuclear weapons proliferation.

Hanford Site and Oak Ridge

Among the pivotal endeavors of the Manhattan Project, the production of plutonium, a rare and highly radioactive element, held immense potential as a key ingredient for the creation of the atomic bomb. Plutonium, today, is mostly man-made. While it does occur naturally, it is rare. Instead, scientists make plutonium using uranium.

Production of plutonium emerged as the next cornerstone in the development of nuclear weapons. This ambitious undertaking unfolded across two significant sites: the Hanford Site in Washington and the bustling town of Oak Ridge, Tennessee.

The journey of plutonium production began with the acquisition of uranium ore from a mine in Ontario. This raw material, extracted from the depths of the earth, would serve as the foundation for the arduous process of creating fissile plutonium.

The Hanford Site in Washington emerged as a critical nucleus for this transformative work, and vast expanses of land were dedicated to the establishment of facilities designed to house reactors and laboratories.

Meanwhile, in Oak Ridge, Tennessee, the pursuit of plutonium production led to the creation of an entire town. Oak Ridge, initially a small farming community, underwent an astonishing transformation as it became an integral part of the Manhattan Project's efforts. The town was chosen for its ideal location, nestled between mountains that offered natural protection in case of disaster.

The scale of the project demanded significant resources, and Oak Ridge swiftly evolved into a bustling hub of scientific innovation and collaboration. Entire communities sprung up around the Hanford Site and Oak Ridge, with individuals from diverse backgrounds converging to contribute to the monumental task at hand.

Ultimately, the collective achievements at Hanford and Oak Ridge were instrumental in the Manhattan Project's success. The transformation of uranium into plutonium marked a critical turning point, demonstrating humanity's ability to manipulate the fundamental building blocks of matter.

Enrichment Challenges

Within the core of the atomic bomb lay the key to its devastating potential: uranium-235, or U-235, a rare isotope capable of initiating the chain reaction of nuclear fission, something we saw Szilard and Fermi do earlier. However, the problem confronting Oppenheimer was that natural uranium predominantly consisted of uranium-238 (U-238), an isotope less conducive to sustaining this reaction. U-235, which they needed, and which would be used for the Little Boy bomb, came in small quantities mixed in with the much larger quantities of U-238.

Working in tandem with the many physicists, engineers, and chemists at the Los Alamos Laboratory, Oppenheimer facilitated the selection and refinement of enrichment methods, and out of their work, a promising path emerged: gaseous diffusion.

In gaseous diffusion, uranium hexafluoride gas is pushed through barriers riddled with minuscule pores. The lighter U-235 atoms traversed these pores slightly faster than their heavier U-238 counterparts, resulting in a concentration of U-235. Meanwhile, gas centrifugation harnessed centrifugal force to segregate isotopes, with the lighter U-235 collecting at the center of rapidly spinning centrifuges.

This was the enrichment process that would be used to develop the Little Boy bomb, while chemical separation was used for the Fat Man bomb, which used plutonium-239 as its fissile material, which is produced in nuclear reactors by irradiating uranium-238 with neutrons. It is then chemically separated from the irradiated uranium and other byproducts.

While it evidently worked out, the journey was fraught with challenges. But Oppenheimer stayed the course. He guided the strategic decisions and fostered collaboration across disciplines. Enrichment demanded an immense quantity of uranium hexafluoride and specialized equipment, and with time constraints dictated by the war, each step was a race against the clock.

And this was just one of the episodes of the saga that was Oppenheimer's life that showed how was able to not just excel on his own, but to generate the energy for an entire team to move. His understanding of theoretical principles, coupled with his visionary leadership, was the force that propelled uranium enrichment forward.

Thin Man

As the project progressed through 1943 and 1944, the scientific teams focused their efforts on developing a prototype known as "Thin Man." This plutonium-based gun-type weapon was designed to function like a firearm, rather than relying on the now-popular implosion mechanism, which relies on precise explosive charges placed around the core to compress the fissile material and trigger a nuclear explosion. However, translating the gun-type concept into a workable reality posed numerous logistical challenges.

It was based on the gun-type mechanism, which would eventually be used for Little Boy. Yet, the divergence lay in the choice of fissile material and the intricate challenges that unfolded. Plutonium-239 posed a unique set of hurdles, chief among them being the phenomenon of pre-initiation. Unlike uranium-235, plutonium-239 was more susceptible to emitting neutrons prematurely, threatening to set off a nuclear chain reaction before the desired configuration was achieved

Critical mass, another crucial factor, further complicated the "Thin Man" design. Plutonium-239 boasted a lower critical mass than uranium-235, presenting both opportunities and challenges. While a smaller critical mass was advantageous for achieving supercritical conditions, it exacerbated the difficulty of assembling sub-critical masses without triggering a premature nuclear reaction.

Another issue was the acceleration of a plutonium bullet inside the bomb. The bullet needed to reach an incredibly high velocity of approximately 3,000 feet per second—to ensure that fission would occur at the right moment, avoiding premature reactions before the bomb's mechanics were ready.

Despite their dedication, the scientists encountered a significant setback. By 1944, it became clear that the gun-type design was fundamentally flawed, as the barrel required for the acceleration of the plutonium bullet would be prohibitively large, making it impractical for transportation within the B-29 Superfortress bombers. This realization led to a difficult decision—Oppenheimer made the call to abandon the Thin Man design in April, 1944.

Setbacks

From the outset, Oppenheimer faced a series of daunting setbacks and challenges. The technical complexity of navigating uncharted territory was overwhelming. Between the need to master the intricacies of uranium and plutonium enrichment, and unraveling the mysteries of nuclear physics, Oppenheimer had his hands full.

Yet, the challenges did not stop there. The project operated under severe resource constraints. Budget limitations forced Oppenheimer to make difficult choices in the allocation of limited resources. They had to prioritize certain aspects of the project over others.

Then there was the issue of security. Not only did the US not want anyone getting a hold of the research, they also did not want to alert the Axis powers of their developments. Security was paramount. The scientists and engineers grappled with the constant threat of espionage and leaks of classified information. The project was cloaked in layers of secrecy, with rigorous background checks and security measures in place to prevent unauthorized access to vital information.

Amidst these tight security concerns, recruiting and managing a diverse group of scientists and engineers posed another challenge. Many of these individuals had strong personalities and differing opinions. Oppenheimer had to navigate the complexities of collaboration and manage interpersonal conflicts to keep the project on track.

Time pressure loomed over Los Alamos. The urgency of World War II demanded rapid progress. The scientists and engineers were under immense pressure to develop the atomic bomb quickly while ensuring the highest safety standards, which led to its own set of challenges and risks.

Working with radioactive materials and highly explosive devices introduced safety concerns. Accidents and mishaps occurred, leading to injuries and a constant need to improve safety protocols.

Yet, perhaps the most profound challenge was the ethical and moral dilemma that weighed on Oppenheimer and his colleagues. They grappled with the realization that they were creating a weapon of mass destruction, one that had the potential to reshape the world. Many scientists had reservations about the consequences of their work, and it raised questions about the long-term impact of their actions.

Through these trials of fire, Kitty was always by his side to provide support, if not by her presence, then through her words when she was afar. Kitty was not always there during the three years he spent at Los Alamos. One of the times she did reside at Los Alamos was when she worked there as a lab technician and gave birth to Katherine Oppenheimer, their daughter, in 1944. When they weren't together, they used letters to communicate.

Kitty and their children were a critical part of Oppenheimer's life, especially during the Manhattan Project, when the literal weight of the world and the cosmos rested on his tired, hungry shoulders. The stress was so high that he would even forget to eat, contributing to his drastic weight loss over the three years he spent at Los Alamos, and thus it is so that her role in supporting Oppenheimer through his Herculean trials, while also raising their children, should not just be a mere note in the margins in the epic of Oppenheimer.

And so with her unbreaking support, he pressed on.

Little Boy

Despite all the setbacks, neither he nor his fellow scientists at Los Alamos were deterred and his leadership was pivotal during this critical phase. He redirected the expertise of the scientists and engineers who had been working on the Thin Man project to a new focus: the development of "Little Boy," a simplified gun-type fission bomb that was to be fueled by enriched uranium-235. Oppenheimer's ability to adapt and reassign resources demonstrated his agility as a leader and his commitment to finding a viable solution.

Even then, the intricate details of bomb design and the interplay of complex factors demanded an exhaustive approach. Oppenheimer, driven by a relentless pursuit of knowledge, tirelessly delved into the technical aspects. It was here that his remarkable ability to grasp the core principles of any subject at lightning speed, which his friend and colleague Hans Bethe recounted, were crucial, especially when considering the drastic need to redesign the gun-type mechanism.

But really, this kind of constant evolution and strategic recalibration was emblematic of the Manhattan Project, not to mention parallel work, which would result in the previously mentioned implosion-type design.

As mentioned earlier, the Little Boy design and the Thin Man design both used the gun-type mechanism, but the former was much more straightforward. Utilizing uranium-235 as its fissile material, Little Boy was composed of two sub-critical masses that were fused using conventional explosives. The merging of these masses would create a supercritical configuration, initiating a nuclear chain reaction that would result in a devastating explosion.

Looking back now, it seems relatively straightforward, their line of progress, but the actual development of both Little Boy and Fat Man, directly under the management of physicist Seth Neddermeyer, was an unimaginable challenge, and within this transformative phase when Oppenheimer and his team were, late into the project, abandoning a design they had worked on for two years, he would bring an expert from the outside to help.

His subsequent invitation to John von Neumann, a Hungarian-born mathematician and physicist, proved instrumental. Von Neumann's intellectual prowess injected fresh vigor into the project by suggesting a spherical shape for implosion-type designs. His revolutionary perspective also introduced the concept of shaped charges, igniting the spark of innovation that would illuminate the path ahead.

As the project embraced the implosion approach, metallurgists rose to the occasion to try and adopt von Neumann's advice, wielding their expertise to cast plutonium into spheres, a crucial component of the Fat Man design. This endeavor was an intricate puzzle in its own right, demanding creative solutions found in the ingenious amalgamation of plutonium with gallium, a breakthrough that facilitated the formation of stable and functional spheres.

Fat Man

As we step away for a moment from the challenges of the gun-type design, we ought to turn our attention to the development of the implosion-type Fat Man, which Oppenheimer actually originally paid less attention to.

As researchers delved into the implosion-type design, they encountered a series of complex challenges that demanded innovative solutions. One of the critical obstacles was achieving a symmetrical implosion – ensuring that the explosive forces acted uniformly from all directions to compress the plutonium core evenly. This was essential to prevent premature initiation and to attain the precise conditions necessary for a successful nuclear detonation.

To accomplish this, the scientists had to carefully engineer the shape and arrangement of the conventional explosive lenses surrounding the plutonium core. These lenses, designed by the previously mentioned Seth Neddermeyer, were meticulously crafted using high-precision techniques, such as shaped charges and hydrodynamic shaping, to shape the explosive shockwaves into a spherical convergence. The success of the implosion hinged on achieving this symmetry with remarkable accuracy, as even slight deviations could lead to a failed detonation or a significantly reduced yield.

Moreover, the implosion design required an intricate synchronization of detonation. The conventional explosives around the core needed to trigger almost simultaneously, creating a shockwave that converged inwards uniformly. This demanded an unprecedented level of precision in timing, which led to the development of innovative detonation mechanisms and electronic circuits capable of achieving microsecond accuracy.

In summary, the implosion design relied on compressing sub-critical masses of fissile material through conventional explosives. This compression initiated a precisely orchestrated sequence of events that led to a supercritical mass, facilitating a controlled and potent nuclear reaction. This approach circumvented the vulnerabilities associated with pre-initiation and critical mass, propelling the implosion-type design towards practicality and reliability.

Trinity

As so it was that as the calendar pages turned to 1945, the culmination of years of tireless labor and intellectual prowess was on the horizon. Two groundbreaking creations, "Little Boy" and "Fat Man," stood as symbols of human ingenuity honed to perfection. Their designs were not merely weapons; they were testaments to the fusion of scientific theory and meticulous engineering.

By mid-1945, the once elusive designs were refined, and the technical challenges that had once seemed insurmountable were gradually overcome. "Little Boy" and "Fat Man" were no longer conceptual constructs; they had been meticulously fashioned into reality through painstaking experimentation and a relentless quest for precision.

The Trinity test, set against the backdrop of the remote desert expanse of the Alamogordo Bombing Range, or the appropriately named Jornada del Muerto, or Journey of the Dead Man, would serve as the crucible in which their work would be validated. In the quiet solitude of the New Mexico landscape, anticipation hung heavy in the air. All their work, all their blood, and all the strength of Oppenheimer's soul was distilled into a single moment—a moment that would redefine the trajectory of human potential.

In the history of science and human innovation, it would mark a pivotal moment. For so many reasons, the stakes of this first and only test were high. A billion dollars, equivalent to about $24 billion today, had been spent on the project, and for one thing, Leslie Groves had made it clear, he did not want to have to explain an effort that cost so much to yield worse than failure to a congressional committee.

As the dawn of the test day broke, on July 16th, 1945, a sense of anticipation hung in the air. Amidst the tense atmosphere, carefully positioned observation shelters lined the cardinal directions, each about 9 kilometers away from the designated blast site. Oppenheimer, Fermi, Bethe, Teller, and von Neumann, were all there, along with several other military officials.

Hushed whispers hung over the early morning, some expressing doubts that the bomb would work at all, let alone deliver the awe-inspiring power that had been hypothesized.

Then, at precisely 5:29 am, the blast occurred, unleashing an explosive energy equivalent to 25 thousand tons of TNT, far greater than all the explosive energy released throughout the entirety of the Second World War until then, combined. A blinding fireball rapidly expanded, painting the desert sky with hues of purple, green, and orange, before coalescing into a brilliant white. The sand around the blast site turned to glass.

Observers who first saw nothing were suddenly captivated by the spectacle of the flash followed by the blinding fireball, their focus drawn to the spectacle unfolding before them as they watched through the goggles which protected their eyes. Then, for the first time in the history of mankind, did those standing miles away witness the first mushroom cloud as it emerged, billowing skyward, eventually reaching the dizzying height of 12 kilometers.

Remarkably, the observers watched all this in silence as the immense noise of the detonation did not reach them for a full 40 seconds after the explosion. It was in the midst of the terribly awesome visual spectacle that the shockwave rippled through the air, its force eventually felt up to 60 miles away - more than an hour's travel by car. Those stationed at the shelters situated 5 miles from the test site recounted an experience akin to standing next to an open oven, as a wave of intense heat washed over them.

Amid the brilliance of the explosion, thoughts raced through the minds of those assembled. For three years, they had toiled in laboratories and research facilities, striving to harness the raw energy of the atom. And in this moment, they witnessed the culmination of their efforts—a monumental testament to human ingenuity and scientific progress. The awe-inspiring display both validated their scientific theories and left them in the blinding light of the immense power they had unleashed.

"If the radiance of a thousand suns were to burst at once into the sky, that would be like the splendor of the mighty one," Oppenheimer had said, quoting the Bhagavad Gita, and encapsulating the boundless, staggering magnitude of the moment.

The general reaction among those present was one of jubilation, even from Oppenheimer. The project had succeeded. The bomb had detonated as intended, and the power it released was more than what they had imagined. The years of tireless research, the collaboration of brilliant minds, and the dedication of countless individuals had borne fruit. The Trinity test not only signaled the achievement of a scientific milestone but also set the stage for a new era—one fraught with ethical questions, geopolitical considerations, and the sobering awareness of the power at humanity's fingertips.

As the mushroom cloud dissipated into the atmosphere, those who bore witness to the event understood that this marked a turning point for humanity. The implications of the successful test would reverberate for decades, shaping the course of history and forever altering our understanding of science, ethics, and the potential for both destruction and innovation.

Chapter 7 Bombings

It wasn't until three weeks later, when the first and only atomic bombs used in war were detonated above Hiroshima and Nagasaki did the full realization of the power they had wrought from the heavens, like Prometheus seizing the fire from the workshop of Athena and Hephaistos on Mount Olympus high above the Earth, strike them.

The main goal of the bombings was to demonstrate the unprecedented and unmatched power the US military now wielded, which could have easily been done by dropping them on deserted islands or on a military target as President Truman had originally intended. But this did not happen, and tragically, it was civilians who were chosen as the target, and the cities of Hiroshima and Nagasaki, left unbombed throughout the firebombing campaign of Japan, were chosen as effective test sites to see just how destructive the atomic bombs were.

The bombings have remained subjects of intense controversy, emblematic of the moral quandaries that can emerge from scientific achievements with dual applications. The attack on Hiroshima, which occurred on August 6, 1945, marked the first use of a nuclear weapon in warfare. The devastation was profound, leveling large sections of the city and causing immediate deaths estimated in the tens of thousands.

While many, including Oppenheimer, publicly at least, accepted the necessity of the bombing of Hiroshima to end the war and save the millions of lives that would have been lost on both sides if America was forced to launch its invasion of the Japanese home islands, the immediate second nuclear attack on

Nagasaki, just three days later was seen by many, Oppenheimer most of all, as absolutely wrong and unacceptable, and provoked widespread condemnation, with unprecedented scale of civilian casualties and the lingering environmental and health consequences from radiation.

The second attack had happened before Japan had had time to process the weight of the first, before they had had time to even consider surrender as a response, when the Japanese people were still reeling with shock of the hellish power that had been unleashed on them.

Rather than being mere demonstrations, the atomic bombings would become the centerpiece of a contentious debate that continues to reverberate.

It is worth noting that the second bombing deeply affected key figures within the Manhattan Project itself, Oppenheimer most of all.

As the one who had played a central role in the project, he was reportedly furious when he learned about the bombing of Nagasaki. Oppenheimer's anger reflected the complex moral dilemmas faced by those who had developed these devastating weapons, and made worse the great ethical battle he had struggled with himself during his three years at Los Alamos, from which he resigned as director two months later on October 16th, 1945. The hollow sorrow and personal responsibility which Oppenheimer felt would determine the rest of his life, which he dedicated with every fiber of his being to peace, pacifism, and the restraint of nuclear weapons development.

Aftermath and Significance

In light of its other consequences, the use of atomic bombs heralded a new era in warfare, where the boundaries of destruction were pushed to previously unimaginable limits. It set in motion a series of reflections on the ethical responsibilities of scientists and governments.

The development of nuclear weapons raised existential threats to humanity while paradoxically ushering in an era of nuclear deterrence, wherein the catastrophic potential of these weapons deterred large-scale conflicts between major powers. This complex legacy underscores the dual nature of scientific advancement and the perpetual need for responsible decision-making.

While many had labeled Oppenheimer as the father of the atomic bomb, a moniker that sticks till this day, it must be stressed that he is, and never was, the monster of a man that label seems to suggest.

In conclusion, the use of atomic bombs over Hiroshima and Nagasaki remains a watershed moment in history, igniting discussions on the morality of employing scientific achievements for destructive purposes. The ethical considerations surrounding these bombings continue to provoke introspection into the responsibilities of both scientists and leaders, as well as the broader implications of harnessing the power of knowledge for the betterment or detriment of humanity, with the rightness and wrongness of how the bombs were used to demonstrate Japan's necessity to surrender continuing to this day.

As for Oppenheimer, it was a few months later when he expressed his heavy regret to President Harry S.

Truman, who had ultimately authorized the use of atomic bombs on Japan, in their first meeting in the Oval Office. This encounter bore witness to the complex moral dilemmas and profound emotions that encompassed the era's historic decisions.

His heart heavy and his conscience even heavier, Oppenheimer said to Truman the chilling phrase, "Mr. President, I have blood on my hands."

This somber declaration encapsulated Oppenheimer's deep remorse and introspection about his involvement in the creation of a weapon that led to immense loss of life and suffering, and bore witness to the unimaginable and indescribable internal conflict and the ethical turmoil he faced in the wake of the atomic bombings, which perhaps no word or phrase even the greatest authors can fashion that would justly encapsulate the feelings that engulfed J. Robert Oppenheimer.

President Truman, on the other hand, responded with a mix of emotions, including anger. He allegedly retorted, "I don't want to hear that again, Bob. I have to make the decisions," and later called him a "crybaby scientist." Truman's response underscored the immense burden of leadership he bore, grappling with decisions that carried profound consequences for humanity, unfortunately not seeing the same things that Oppenheimer considered.

The exchange between Oppenheimer and Truman serves as a poignant reminder that history's most significant moments are often shaped not only by grand decisions but also by the personal reflections and interactions of those who play pivotal roles.

Legacy and Ethical Implications of the Manhattan Project

Looking back on the Manhattan Project, there is no denying the profound destructive force that was unleashed, nor the immeasurable sorrow at the reckless loss of life that occurred on August 6th and 9th respectively. With debates on whether the indiscriminate killing of civilians could justify preventing the outcome thought to take place should the bombs have been deployed differently, the Manhattan Project and the development of nuclear weapons gave rise to a whole new era of diplomacy, war, strategy, and global ideology.

With the end of the Second World War and the beginning of the Cold War, nuclear weapons defined the power balances and conflicts that spanned the second half of the 20th century and early 21st. To that effect, the prospect of war, once a common occurrence, was significantly reduced, for the world grew aware of the possibility of escalation to nuclear confrontation.

It is thus that the work of Oppenheimer goes far beyond the tragedy of Hiroshima and Nagasaki. By the establishment of nuclear deterrence, and the notion of nuclear peace, where the threat of nuclear war holds nations back from engaging at all, the most destructive weapons in history paradoxically gave rise to the decline in conflicts that followed the end of the Second World War.

This notion of nuclear deterrence and mutually assured destruction, also ironically abbreviated as MAD, gave rise to an intricate geopolitical dance. The superpowers built up their nuclear arsenals not with the intention of using them, but as symbols of their strength and a guarantee of their security. The world held its breath as political tensions escalated, knowing that any misstep could trigger a cataclysmic chain of events. In this backdrop, the debate shifted from centering only on the morality of using nuclear weapons to include the ethics of possessing and threatening their use.

But nonetheless, nuclear power reduced the prospect of war. And that is what should be considered part of Oppenheimer's legacy.

In retrospect, the legacy of the Manhattan Project raises deep ethical questions that persist to this day. The scientists and leaders who steered the project were thrust into a maelstrom of unprecedented moral complexity. Their work yielded both immense power and the potential for annihilation. The world witnessed the paradox that scientific progress, while a testament to human ingenuity, could also plunge humanity into the abyss.

As the international community navigates the 21st century, the ethical lessons of the Manhattan Project remain vital. The specter of nuclear conflict still looms, but the lessons learned from history's precipice should guide us towards a world where the pursuit of knowledge and progress is tempered by a vigilant consideration of the ethical implications. It is a reminder that scientific achievements must always be accompanied by a deep sense of responsibility for the consequences they unleash.

Chapter 8 His Philosophy & Atoms for Peace

"The people of this world must unite or they will perish."
J. Robert Oppenheimer

In the shadow of mushroom clouds that erupted as a direct result of Oppenheimer's work on the Manhattan Project and the depths of the emotional and ethical turmoil that accompanied him during that time is perhaps no better opportunity to address the philosophy of Oppenheimer.

As alluded to in previous chapters, he saw the worth and value of the philosophical, as much as he appreciated the importance and significance of the tangible. This, combined with his humanist values of ethics and compassion instilled during his childhood, undoubtedly made the weight of his work that much more painful to bear.

And it was during his work on the Manhattan Project that he found in the Bhagavad Gita, or The Lord's Song, the 700-verse poem that is one of Hinduism's most sacred texts, a way to interpret his actions.

The words he read in that 2000-year-old epic would go on to have a profound effect upon his life and way of thinking, and he himself named it, together with T.S. Eliot's *The Waste Land*, on the tragedy and sorrow of loss and brokenness, especially in the context of the First World War and itself based on the Upanishad, another one of Hinduism's greatest epics, as one of the texts that shaped his life.

As he said, "I have read the Greeks. I find the Hindus deeper."

Having already been saturated with the Greek and Latin classics of ancient times while at Harvard, his philosophical journey was well underway, and his venture into Eastern philosophy was about to begin, deeper than what he had touched on during his college years. While teaching physics at Berkeley, he had studied Sanskrit under Professor Arthur W. Ryder, who had introduced the language to him.

Taking private lessons on Thursday evenings, Oppenheimer wrote to his brother, Frank, "I am learning Sanskrit, enjoying it very much and enjoying again the sweet luxury of being taught". It was here that he was introduced to the Gita, which he later called "the most beautiful philosophical song existing in any known tongue," and would keep a copy with him at all times, the one now housed in the Bradbury Science Museum in the Los Alamos Laboratory, while handing out several to all his friends and colleagues.

Oppenheimer's friends thought his obsession with an Indian language was weird, but Harold F. Cherniss, one of his biographers, said that it actually made "perfect sense", as Oppenheimer was a man with a "taste of the mystical and the cryptic".

And so armed as he was with the knowledge to read and understand one of the oldest languages in existence, Oppenheimer went on to immerse himself in the Bhagavad Gita, a process that was never complete and like the study of all great works, could perhaps never be. It was a constant, reflective, iterative journey of understanding for Oppenheimer as he read the Gita over and over again. Its teachings were presented as a conversation written in eloquent prose between the god of creation, protection, and transformation Vishnu, disguised as Krishna, and an archer named Arjuna, who does not wish to take part in a war in which his own relatives are among the enemy's ranks, and talked of duty and people's roles in the vast scale of the cosmos, something that Oppenheimer grappled with especially during the Manhattan Project and his central role in creating a weapon that incinerated tens of thousands in the blink of an eye.

In a summary that falls short of the weight of the Gita's words, Krishna advised Arjuna that all he did and should do was in accordance with his *dharma*, a word that finds no English translation close enough to do it justice, other than duty. Oppenheimer likely understood that this advice did not apply only to warriors and those caught up in war, but to all people. The Bhagavad Gita focuses on how one can best follow their *dharma*, and the dilemma Arjuna finds himself in is much like the one Oppenheimer was dropped into by the Manhattan Project. Arjuna was thrown into a Great War that would continue to rage whether he took part in it or not, just like Oppenheimer was. And the questions that gnawed at him of how he could fight, and kill, while also acknowledging the Oneness of all sentient beings, also resonated with the physicist.

Non-dualism, which considers that destruction and creation are not opposites, but rather are part of all life, and which the Bhagavad Gita discusses, is something that no doubt influenced Oppenheimer greatly. And with his enormous care for right over wrong, and good over evil, in a world faced with the horrors of the Nazi regime and the Imperial war machine, his *dharma* had long ago developed as doing good for humanity, thus helping us to comprehend, and perhaps even helped himself to reason his own willingness and central work in advancing the development of the nuclear bomb. Oppenheimer was following what he believed to be his duty. To take it a step further, the historian James Hijiya posits a unique perspective that Oppenheimer's great concern for duty helped him to separate his own from what happened after, that he saw his scientific work as separate from how the government might choose to use it.

One account Hijiya cites as proof of this was how when Oppenheimer was being forced to name potential security risks at the Los Alamos Laboratory by an Army intelligence officer, he told the man, "That's your duty.... My duty is not to implicate these people.... My duty is to protect them."

Even if his claim is true, it still does not subtract from the grief he carried in the wake of the atomic bombings, even decades afterward.

In light of the idea that Oppenheimer placed enormous significance on the value of duty, it is not contradictory or confusing then to note that in the wake of the atomic age and the rise of nuclear weapons that he ushered in, he returned to his pacifist self and campaigned with every fiber of his being to have the devastating forces he had unleashed restrained. Because once the war was over, Oppenheimer's duty, his *dharma*, reverted fully back to what it was before the Manhattan Project. The pursuit of scientific progress, peace, and justice for humanity.

Still, it would be horribly irresponsible to use this to color Oppenheimer as a cold figure who saw the death of hundreds of thousands that were a direct result of his work as nothing more than the carrying out of his duty. The weight of those lives lost, snuffed out in an instant by the forces of nature he had helped weaponize, weighed on him for the rest of his life, perhaps far heavier than we can ever know.

But, we may yet have a glimpse.

When he said, "I am become Death. The destroyer of worlds," in his 1965 interview with NBC News twenty years after the Trinity test and the bombings of Hiroshima and Nagasaki, he added," I suppose we all thought that, one way or another." Oppenheimer's solemn recognition of the destruction he had helped bring about is clear.

He also said, in another interview with the Times, that "he never regretted, and do not regret now, having done my part of the job." No doubt that was true, in so far as that meant doing his duty and securing the forces of good in a world where humanity was facing off against those of darkness, the terrible and awesome--in its truest sense of the word, power of the atom, that would surely have used it to the utter destruction of humankind. In that we can be sure, Oppenheimer did his duty.

We can also be sure that the moral and existential dilemmas that plagued Oppenheimer during his years at Los Alamos and for the rest of his life was an extremely complicated and multi-faceted one, whose reasoning he no doubt struggled with, and in which the concepts encapsulated in the verses of the *Bhagavad Gita* played a significant role in helping Oppenheimer interpret his own quandary.

And of one more thing we can be certain, is that we will never fully comprehend, maybe not even fully imagine, the scope of great conflict that raged within his heart and soul, an ironic parallel to the conflict that pushed him to deal with such questions in the first place, and for which was perhaps ultimately his only reason for developing the bomb.

Nuclear Activism

An embodiment of his pacifist and peace-oriented vision was seen in his involvement with the General Advisory Committee of the United States Atomic Energy Commission. As chairman of the AEC's scientific arm, Oppenheimer played a role in advising the government on matters related to nuclear policy, advocating for responsible development and control of nuclear technology.

Amid the backdrop of his advocacy for peaceful scientific advancement, Oppenheimer's stance on nuclear weapons after World War II carried profound ethical weight. He had played a central role in the development of the atomic bomb through the Manhattan Project, and had firsthand experience of the unprecedented destruction these weapons could unleash.

Oppenheimer's position on nuclear weapons evolved into one of caution and reflection. He voiced his concerns about the rapid proliferation of nuclear arsenals, advocating for international controls and treaties to prevent the catastrophic use of these weapons. His awareness of the potential consequences, coupled with his advocacy for international collaboration, underscored his commitment to using science as a force for good rather than destruction.

The Acheson-Lilienthal Report: Pioneering International Control of Atomic Energy

The year was 1945, and the world was still reeling from the unimaginable horrors of Hiroshima and Nagasaki, cities reduced to ashes by the unprecedented destructive power of nuclear weapons. As the dust settled on the aftermath of World War II, a profound shift in thinking about atomic energy emerged, led by none other than the man who had developed history's first nuclear weapons.

Oppenheimer had witnessed the devastation firsthand, and he was acutely aware of the urgent need to prevent the unbridled spread of nuclear weapons. His vision for international control of atomic energy found its expression in the Acheson-Lilienthal Report, a landmark document that would shape the course of history.

The context was one of global uncertainty. The United States, having harnessed the power of atomic bombs, recognized the immense responsibility that came with this knowledge. The Soviet Union's successful testing of its atomic bomb in 1949 added fuel to the fire of Cold War tensions. It was against this backdrop that the United States turned to experts like Oppenheimer for guidance.

The report's name bears the imprints of two key architects: Dean Acheson, the then-US Under Secretary of State, and David Lilienthal, the inaugural chairman of the US Atomic Energy Commission. Working in concert with input from Oppenheimer and other leading minds, they forged a vision that would change the course of nuclear history.

At its heart, the Acheson-Lilienthal Report championed the idea of international control. It proposed the establishment of the Atomic Development Authority, endowed with sweeping powers. This authority would oversee all facets of atomic energy, from the production of fissile materials like uranium and plutonium to their use for peaceful purposes, while keeping a vigilant eye on their diversion for military ends.

The report's boldest proposition was perhaps the notion that atomic energy should be considered a global resource, owned collectively by all nations. It represented a significant departure from the prevailing belief that only a select few nuclear-armed states should have dominion over this extraordinary power.

Amidst the tumultuous Cold War climate, the report also advocated for gradual disarmament. While acknowledging the complexity of complete disarmament, it urged a reduction in the number of nuclear weapons as a critical step toward global stability.

To ensure accountability and compliance, the report recommended a system of inspections and verification. Transparency and trust-building were deemed essential elements of any successful control regime.

The Acheson-Lilienthal Report left an indelible mark on history. While not immediately adopted in its entirety, its ideas laid the foundation for subsequent initiatives and agreements. In 1957, the International Atomic Energy Agency (IAEA) emerged, charged with promoting the peaceful utilization of nuclear technology and preventing the dangerous proliferation of nuclear weapons.

In retrospect, the Acheson-Lilienthal Report marked a pivotal moment when the world began to recognize the imperative of international cooperation and control to temper the perilous potential of atomic energy. Its enduring legacy continues to shape global efforts, striking a delicate balance between the benefits of nuclear technology and the paramount need for nuclear security.

Oppenheimer's Urgent Plea for Nuclear Diplomacy

It was the early 1950s, and the world was perched on the precipice of a perilous nuclear age. J. Robert Oppenheimer, the man behind the Manhattan Project, had a grave concern that weighed heavily on his mind – the unchecked proliferation of nuclear weapons. As the Cold War cast its shadow, Oppenheimer knew that decisive action was needed to prevent catastrophe.

Oppenheimer was no ordinary scientist; he was a visionary thinker who understood the catastrophic power of atomic weapons all too well. He believed that the United States had a moral and strategic obligation to lead the world away from the brink of nuclear annihilation. To achieve this, he knew he had to reach the ears of the most powerful man in the country: President Dwight D. Eisenhower.

The consultations began in earnest. Oppenheimer, with his deep expertise in nuclear physics and an acute sense of the global stakes, met with Eisenhower on multiple occasions. Their discussions were not casual chit-chats but intense and weighty deliberations on the future of nuclear policy.

Oppenheimer impressed upon Eisenhower the urgency of the situation. The world had witnessed the terrifying destructive potential of atomic bombs in

Hiroshima and Nagasaki. The Soviet Union's successful testing of its atomic bomb in 1949 had heightened Cold War tensions to a fever pitch. The two superpowers were engaged in a dangerous arms race, stockpiling nuclear arsenals that could obliterate entire cities.

Oppenheimer's message was clear: the status quo was unsustainable. The world needed a new approach, one that prioritized international cooperation over the reckless pursuit of nuclear dominance. He believed that the United States should take a bold and unprecedented step – a step that would change the course of history.

Oppenheimer's vision found a receptive ear in Eisenhower. The President shared his concerns about the nuclear arms race and the need to find a way to bring it under control. The consultations were not just academic discussions; they were the crucible where a new approach to nuclear diplomacy was forged.

The result of these intense deliberations was the Atoms for Peace initiative. In his historic speech to the United Nations in 1953, Eisenhower laid out a visionary plan that echoed the sentiments of Oppenheimer. The president creating the IAEA, the International Atomic Energy Agency, to oversee the peaceful use of atomic energy worldwide. It was a dramatic departure from the Cold War narrative of mutually assured destruction.

Oppenheimer's influence on Eisenhower was undeniable. The scientist had pressed the importance of international cooperation, of openness, trust and transparency in age fraught with secrecy and suspicion, the responsible use of atomic energy, and the necessity of preventing runaway nuclear proliferation. These ideas were not just academic theories; they were the catalysts for a seismic shift in US nuclear policy.

In the end, Oppenheimer's consultations with Eisenhower bore fruit in the form of the Atoms for Peace initiative, a testament to the power of science and diplomacy to chart a safer course in a world teetering on the edge of nuclear abyss.

Chapter 9 Betrayed

"And we know that as long as men are free to ask what they must,
free to say what they think, free to think what they will,
freedom can never be lost, and science can never regress."
J. Robert Oppenheimer

The poignant tragedy of Oppenheimer's life then was far from over, and was about to get worse.

In the early 1950s, the United States found itself in the grip of an era marked by paranoia, suspicion, and an intense fear of communism that resulted in excesses and hysteria. This period, known as McCarthyism, was characterized by the rampant anti-communist crusade that had turned into a mechanism of political persecution and ideological enforcement, casting a long and dark shadow over American society.

At the heart of McCarthyism was Senator Joseph McCarthy, an insidiously charismatic and ruthless demagogue who exploited the nation's anxiety about the Cold War and the spread of communism to gain power. With the Cold War's escalating tensions that had cast a chill over the world, dividing nations into ideological blocs and sparking fears of infiltration and espionage, it was easy for McCarthy to gain power.

McCarthy abused the imperative need to resist communism by leveraging it as a potent tool for advancing his own political agenda. He capitalized on the genuine concerns of the American people regarding the potential infiltration of communist ideology within the nation's institutions and his actions very nearly succeeded in tearing them to ground.

McCarthy's misguided actions began in 1950 when he claimed to possess a list of 205 individuals in the U.S. State Department who were allegedly members of the Communist Party and agents of the Soviet Union. Although McCarthy's list was never substantiated, and he never released it, it ignited a fervor of suspicion that spread like wildfire throughout the country.

The fear of communist infiltration had a profound impact on American institutions, particularly in the realms of entertainment, government, and education. The first of those three were among the first to feel the effects of McCarthyism, as Hollywood became a target for accusations of harboring communist sympathizers.

The House Un-American Activities Committee, or HUAC, summoned numerous actors, directors, and writers to testify about their political beliefs, affiliations, and associations. Those who refused to cooperate or were perceived as uncooperative were jailed for contempt or more often blacklisted, effectively ending their careers.

This period of ideological and political enforcement stifled artistic freedom and led to an era of self-censorship, as individuals feared retribution for expressing dissenting views, and the irreparable damage it would do to their lives and the lives of their friends and family.

In the realm of government, the witch hunt for suspected communists reached a fever pitch. Loyalty oaths were demanded of government employees, and any perceived deviation from the prevailing anti-communist sentiment could result in immediate dismissal.

The case of Alger Hiss, a former State Department official accused of espionage, exemplified the extent to which McCarthyism could be used for political persecution. Although Hiss's guilt was never conclusively proven, he was convicted of perjury in a trial that was more a result of anti-communist fervor than concrete evidence.

The educational sector also fell victim to the ideological fervor of McCarthyism. Professors, researchers, and intellectuals were scrutinized for their political beliefs, and educators deemed to have communist sympathies were subjected to public humiliation and job loss. This not only silenced dissent within academia but also impeded the free exchange of ideas that was essential for intellectual growth and progress. This effect was also felt in the professional world, including bar and medical associations.

The media's role was complex in the dissemination of McCarthyism. Some newspapers and broadcasters supported McCarthy's crusade, amplifying his claims and fanning the flames of fear. However, a handful of journalists, most notably Edward R. Murrow, emerged as a voice of reason, challenging McCarthy's tactics and demanding evidence for his accusations. Murrow's televised criticism of McCarthy marked a turning point in public opinion, gradually eroding the senator's influence and exposing the dangers of unchecked power.

It wasn't until the Senate's televised Army-McCarthy hearings in 1954 that McCarthy's reign of terror began to unravel. The hearings, part of McCarthy's rampaging investigations of communist influence in the US Army, showcased his bullying tactics and lack of evidence. The televised spectacle turned public sentiment overwhelmingly against McCarthy, leading to his censure by the Senate and a subsequent rapid decline in his influence.

The era of McCarthyism serves as a cautionary tale about the consequences of allowing fear and paranoia to dictate political and social discourse. It demonstrated how unchecked power could erode civil liberties, suppress dissenting voices, and pervert justice in the name of ideological enforcement. McCarthy's manipulation of the need to resist communism for personal gain underscores the importance of maintaining a vigilant and informed citizenry to safeguard democratic values and prevent the abuse of power.

***

It was thus amid the tumultuous currents of the Second Red Scare that one of the most remarkable and tragic stories unfolded—the tale of Oppenheimer and the tarnishing of his reputation, public standing, and legacy. It was nothing less than a complete character assassination of a man who had played an instrumental role in the Manhattan Project, contributing to America's victory in World War II and reshaping the course of history. He found himself swept up by the tide of McCarthyism, despite his significant and historic service to the nation.

Fueled by McCarthy's rhetoric the events that followed cast a long and ominous shadow over Oppenheimer's legacy and his future. This intersection of history and paranoia, of personal conviction and political agendas, would come to define one of the darkest chapters of Oppenheimer's life.

Oppenheimer's accomplishments were undeniable. Beyond his role in the Manhattan Project and pivotal contribution to ending the Second World War, he had made substantial contributions to the fields of theoretical physics and quantum mechanics, laying the groundwork for our current comprehension of existence. His brilliance was matched only by his sense of duty, and his service to the nation had been unquestionable. However, as the Cold War unfolded and the specter of communism loomed large, his past affiliations and associations with communist movements were used against him to tarnish his reputation.

As mentioned in previous chapters, the 1930s had seen Oppenheimer aligning himself with progressive and left-wing organizations, spurred by the rising menace of fascism in Europe. The appeal of socialism, seen as a counterpoint to the encroaching darkness, had drawn him to causes that championed civil liberties and social justice, not to mention his relationship with Jean Tatlock, and his brother, Frank, and friends and students, several of whom were registered members of the Communist Party of the United States of America, as well as his wife, Katherine.

While Oppenheimer himself had never joined the CPUSA, these connections became a focal point of scrutiny when he was brought before the House Un-American Activities Committee (HUAC) in 1949, when Frank was being investigated for his Communist membership, for which Frank was blacklisted, effectively barred from scientific research, and his passport was confiscated, preventing him from working abroad.

For Robert, this was a critical moment in the trajectory of his life—an encounter that would lead to the profound altering of his relationship with the nation he had served so dutifully, to a notion of betrayal. Yet, this did not diminish either his loyalty or patriotism. As he said, "Dammit, I happen to love this country."

The HUAC proceedings forced Oppenheimer to acknowledge his past ties to the Communist Party and to admit that some of his Berkeley students had been members. Though he asserted that he himself had never formally joined the party, the atmosphere of fear and suspicion that gripped the nation often turned mere associations into damning evidence. The very ideals that had once motivated his commitment to leftist and connection with communist causes were now being used to cast a shadow of doubt over his loyalty.

As the 1950s dawned, the clouds of suspicion only grew darker. The Federal Bureau of Investigation harbored suspicions, albeit misguided, that Oppenheimer might be a Soviet spy. The chair of the Atomic Energy Commission, the AEC, Lewis Strauss, played a pivotal role in revoking Oppenheimer's security clearance, leaving him stripped of the trust he had earned through his wartime contributions. The man who had been integral to the birth of the atomic age was now treated as a potential threat to national security, in utter contempt for the great services he had rendered.

It all started when an ominous letter emerged as a damning testament to the allegations swirling around Oppenheimer. William Liscum Borden, a former executive director of Congress' Joint Atomic Energy Committee, penned the letter to J. Edgar Hoover, then the director of the FBI, in which he claimed that "more probably than not J. Robert Oppenheimer is an agent of the Soviet Union."

This letter was riddled with unsubstantiated claims such as possible ties to Nazism because of his German heritage. It also claimed that he was in frequent contact with Soviet agents and that he had lied several times to Major General Leslie Groves and the FBI about his communist associations. These, among other baseless accusations, greatly fueled by the pervasive paranoia of the era defined by McCarthyism, further stoked the flames of suspicion around Oppenheimer.

The consequent suspicion against him was passed on to President Eisenhower, who from then on excluded him from top-secret discussions about America's nuclear development, as Oppenheimer had been part of and central to since the Manhattan Project.

To understand the significance of these events, one must delve into the complex relationships and motivations at play. Oppenheimer's strong opposition to the development of the hydrogen bomb, a weapon exponentially more destructive than the atomic bomb, had set him on a collision course with some of his former colleagues and political power players. Edward Teller, once a close friend and colleague of Oppenheimer during the Manhattan Project, played a pivotal role in the development of the hydrogen bomb. Oppenheimer's ethical reservations about this new weapon strained their relationship. Teller's staunch support for the hydrogen bomb placed him at odds with Oppenheimer's stance, eventually leading to a profound rift between the two.

Meanwhile, Lewis Strauss had emerged as a staunch advocate for the development of thermonuclear weapons such as the hydrogen bomb. Oppenheimer's opposition to this project and his influence within atomic circles put him in direct conflict with Strauss' vision for American nuclear supremacy. Their tense relationship, caused by a perceived humiliation on the part of Strauss, created an environment ripe for conflict, with Strauss holding both personal and ideological motivations to discredit Oppenheimer.

The confluence of personal vendettas, differing political agendas, and the climate of fear and hysteria accordingly created a perfect storm that culminated in Oppenheimer's hearing, which he demanded, as was his right, when Strauss told him it had been revoked and advised him to resign. This closed hearing, held in late spring of the following year, beginning on April 12th, 1954, marked a turning point in his life. Former colleagues and friends were called to testify, among them Edward Teller. To the shock of many, Teller's testimony portrayed Oppenheimer's behavior during his tenure as the director of the Los Alamos Laboratory as questionable. The man who had once been his close associate was now instrumental in casting doubt upon his character.

The proceedings of this hearing resulted in Oppenheimer definitively losing his security clearance and his standing tarnished. It was a devastating blow, not only to him personally but also to the nation's scientific and ethical fabric. This part of Oppenheimer's story, encompassing personal allegiances and political maneuvering, is emblematic of an era where fear and suspicion too often overruled reason and justice. His ordeal underscores the enduring need to guard against the corrosive power of blind paranoia and the perilous consequences of sacrificing principles for the sake of political agendas.

Consequences

The aftermath of Oppenheimer's 1954 security hearing marked a period of profound turmoil and personal devastation. The man who had played a pivotal role in the development of the atomic bomb and the shaping of the modern scientific landscape found himself facing a future that was unrecognizable from the one he had envisioned, and the years that followed the security hearing and its surrounding ills were, by all accounts, excruciatingly difficult for Oppenheimer.

The weight of the accusations and suspicions that had been cast upon him weighed heavily on his shoulders, burdening him with a sense of disillusionment and betrayal. The country he had devoted his intellect to, the nation he had served with unwavering dedication during World War II, had now turned its gaze upon him with suspicion and doubt.

As news of the security hearing spread, the academic community's reaction was odd. It was a response that mirrored the complexity of Oppenheimer's situation. Though many of his colleagues and those he knew did rally to his defense, recognizing the absurdity of labeling a man of his stature and integrity as a security risk. They saw through the political posturing and recognized the injustice that was being inflicted upon a man who had dedicated his life to the pursuit of knowledge and the advancement of science.

Yet, even within the folds of support, there was an air of caution. The rest of the academic community's response was indicative of the uncertain times. The specter of McCarthyism loomed large, casting a chilling effect on the freedoms of thought and expression. Those who dared to speak out in support of Oppenheimer risked being labeled as sympathizers or worse, facing their own reckoning with the zealous witch hunts of the era.

For Oppenheimer, this response was both heartening and heartbreaking. While he undoubtedly drew strength from the solidarity of his peers, he also witnessed the academic community's vulnerability to the prevailing political climate. The halls of intellectual pursuit, where ideas were meant to flourish and debate was meant to thrive, had become entangled in a web of fear, suspicion, and politics. In chains.

The combination of these factors—Oppenheimer's personal anguish over the trial's outcome and the precarious state of intellectual discourse—rendered this period one of somber reflection and shattered illusions. The man who had once been a beacon of scientific brilliance found himself navigating the wreckage of his own reputation, surrounded by the fragments of a life that had been irrevocably altered.

Perhaps one of the most poignant consequences of Oppenheimer's ordeal was his decision to step back from significant endeavors aimed at promoting international awareness of the dangers of nuclear proliferation. Collaborative efforts led by prominent figures like Albert Einstein sought to sound the alarm about the perils of unchecked nuclear arms races and the potential for global catastrophe. However, Oppenheimer's own personal crisis had led him to reassess his place in such endeavors, and to not attach his name to movements, lest his baggage taint it.

The combination of political scrutiny, personal betrayal, and the shifting sands of his convictions thus left Oppenheimer in a state of ambivalence. While his expertise and experience could have contributed significantly to these initiatives, he opted to distance himself from the forefront of these campaigns. He chose, instead, to find solace and reflection away from the mainland United States, seeking refuge in the tranquil surroundings of the Virgin Islands.

Oppenheimer's retreat to an estate on Gibney Beach, located on the island of St. John, marked a symbolic departure from the scientific and political arenas that had once defined his life. Here, amid the gentle lapping of the ocean waves and the rustling of palm trees, he sought respite from the turbulent currents of controversy that had engulfed him. The beachside estate, which would later bear his name colloquially as "Oppenheimer Beach," became his sanctuary—a space where he could grapple with his shattered confidence and chart a new course forward.

The decision to seclude himself from the heart of scientific and political discourse was undoubtedly a deeply introspective one, and can be seen as an act of self-preservation, a way to shield himself from the relentless public scrutiny and rebuild his sense of self away from the prying eyes of a nation that had, in many ways, let him down. But while he may have stepped away from the forefront of international efforts to curb nuclear proliferation, his impact on the scientific community and the course of history could not be erased.

However, one notable turning point in this part of Oppenheimer's journey was the recognition he received from abroad. Despite the skepticism and suspicion that had colored his reputation within his own country, the international scientific community recognized the significance of his contributions. In 1957, the French government awarded Oppenheimer the prestigious *Legion d'Honneur*, or the Legion of Honor, France's highest commendation that symbolized his contributions to the Allied cause during World War II. This gesture from a foreign nation highlighted the dissonance between the way he was perceived at home and the esteem he commanded on the global stage.

Equally significant was Oppenheimer's recognition by the United Kingdom. In 1962, he was made a foreign member of the Royal Society, one of the world's most prestigious scientific organizations. This honor not only reflected the broader international acknowledgment of his scientific achievements but also underscored the fact that his work transcended national boundaries. By recognizing him as a foreign member, the Royal Society conveyed that the pursuit of scientific knowledge and understanding should be celebrated and valued regardless of political controversies.

Moreover, these international acknowledgments evolved into being part of a larger narrative that was unfolding within the United States itself. With the decline of McCarthy and the chaos he had created subsiding by the dawn of the 1960s, the country was beginning to reckon with the excesses of McCarthyism and the Second Red Scare, realizing that many individuals had been unfairly targeted and their reputations tarnished by political hysteria. As this collective realization took hold, figures like Oppenheimer, who had been unjustly accused, began to experience a slow but steady shift in public perception.

All this, together with the international recognition and attempts at rehabilitation culminated in another pivotal moment for Oppenheimer's legacy. In 1963, President John F. Kennedy invited him to the White House during a gathering of Nobel laureates as an apologetic gesture for how the US government had outcast him.

In 1965, two years later, President Lyndon B. Johnson awarded him the Enrico Fermi Award, which had been established by the US Department of Energy to honor significant contributions to nuclear science and technology, and had already been presented to John von

Neumann in 1946, Hans Bethe in 1961, and Edward Teller in 1962. While this award was certainly belated, it carried immense symbolic weight. It was not only an acknowledgment of Oppenheimer's past contributions but also a tacit admission of the government's previous misjudgments.

In many ways, these international acknowledgments and awards were not just about Oppenheimer himself; they were indicative of the broader healing process occurring within American society. The recognition from other countries and the acknowledgment of his value by his peers were part of a collective effort to rectify the injustices of the past and restore the honor of those who had been unjustly targeted.

Chapter 10 Ascent to the Stars

"Confidence thrives on honesty, on honor, on the sacredness of obligations, on faithful protection and on unselfish performance. Without them it cannot live."
Franklin D. Roosevelt

But even as the world began the great project of recognizing his contributions and his country attempted to restore the reputation it had destroyed, in 1965, a shadow fell over J. Robert Oppenheimer with his diagnosis of throat cancer. The timing of his illness seemed almost poetic, sandwiched between his embattled reputation and the international recognition of his scientific contributions. That's even more so when we remember that Oppenheimer's life was one marked always by conundrums and ironies.

The very man who had wielded his intellect to shape the course of history was now confronted with a formidable adversary caused by his excessive smoking. This diagnosis marked a somber twist in the tale of a brilliant mind, hinting at the complexities that life weaves even for the most exceptional individuals.

His ailment carried its own weight of irony. Oppenheimer, the scientist who had delved into the intricate workings of the atomic world, now found himself confronting the harsh realities of his own body's molecular composition, ravaged by carcinogenic forces.

The treatment options, though advanced for the time, still meant that Oppenheimer had to endure the grueling trials of major chemotherapy after a surgical attempt to remove it failed. The very same spirit that had pushed him to unravel the mysteries of the universe now faced a different kind of test—endurance in the face of relentless medical procedures.

As Oppenheimer underwent chemotherapy, his journey echoed the larger themes of his life—a man of contradictions, whose intellectual prowess was equally matched by personal vulnerabilities. And while the Enrico Fermi Award symbolized the potential for redemption and a glimmer of appreciation for the great sacrifices he had made for his country, it was his physical battle with cancer that mirrored the resilience emblematic of his pursuit of truth.

Sadly, after months of agony, Oppenheimer passed away in his sleep on February 16th, 1967, in his home in Princeton.

A week later, his memorial was held in Alexander Hall, on the sprawling campus of Princeton University.

On the day of the funeral, the somber skies seemed to mirror the collective grief felt by the six hundred attendees who gathered to honor Oppenheimer's memory, besides his brother Frank, who had witnessed his journey from his earliest days, his children and his wife Kitty to whom he had been married for nearly three decades by then and who had been by his side through thick and thin.

The assembly comprised a constellation of luminaries from the scientific, political, and military spheres, each an embodiment of the far-reaching influence Oppenheimer had cultivated throughout his lifetime.

Among the distinguished attendees were figures who had shared in his triumphs and challenges. Hans Bethe, the distinguished physicist and his fellow colleague who had known him since he was a professor at Caltech, Leslie Groves, the resolute military leader who orchestrated the Manhattan Project and had stood by his side even during his security hearing, George F. Kennan, the diplomat whose insights shaped American foreign policy, Henry DeWolf Smyth, the authoritative author of the famed "Smyth Report" that delineated the Manhattan Project, and Eugene Wigner, the mathematician and physicist who was one of Oppenheimer's closest friends.

Renowned historian Arthur M. Schlesinger, Jr. was also in attendance, as was the celebrated novelist John O'Hara, both paying their respects to the multifaceted legacy of the man who loved the arts as much as did the intricacies of science. Notably, George Balanchine, the luminary behind the New York City Ballet, also stood among the attendees, a testament to Oppenheimer's broad cultural impact. They were just a few of the people from so many backgrounds that Oppenheimer's influence had reached.

The commemorative service was punctuated by heartfelt eulogies delivered by Hans Bethe, George Kennan and Henry Smyth. Bethe, in his remarks, painted a vivid picture of the intellectual synergy he shared with Oppenheimer, encapsulating the profound mutual respect they held for each other, while Kennan spoke eloquently about the immense responsibilities and moral dilemmas that Oppenheimer grappled with during the Manhattan Project, Henry speaking to his dedication and leadership.

Following their eulogies, Oppenheimer's body was cremated, an act that symbolized his transformation from the physical realm into the realm of memory and ideas that would continue to shape the world. His ashes were placed into a humble urn, a vessel that held the essence of his unparalleled intellect and legacy.

Later, in a poignant and symbolic gesture, Kitty, his widow, would let the urn slip from her grasp, releasing the ashes into the sea with their St. John beach house in sight, which, among other things, he had left to her and their children in his will.

In honor of his indomitable spirit that defied the boundaries of mortality, his departure to the ocean, near the place he held dear, encapsulated the eternal cycle of life.

The funeral of J. Robert Oppenheimer underscored the great reverence held for him by those who knew him closely and those who admired him from afar. It was also a resounding tribute to a man whose contributions reverberated across disciplines, nations, and generations, continuing to do so today.

Nobel Prize

In the wake of Oppenheimer's immeasurable impact and significance that extended far beyond his work on the Manhattan Project - such as, though by far not limited to, his groundbreaking contributions to the development of molecular physics through the Born-Oppenheimer Approximation and his work on the science of black holes and neutron stars, we are forced to question why he was never awarded the Nobel Prize. For making great strides in the advancement of our understanding of the cosmos and of existence itself, he was never fully recognized.

Though having been nominated multiple times, once in 1947, again in 1951, and once more in 1967, he was never awarded. This puzzle of why despite his monumental contributions to science and society, continues to captivate historians, scholars, and the scientific community with the question of whether he did or did not deserve one.

The Nobel Prize has historically been bestowed upon individuals for specific groundbreaking achievements, which Oppenheimer certainly had, and while he was nominated several times, it was the collaborative and managerial nature of his work that partly kept him from winning.

One other significant factor that also differentiated Oppenheimer from some of his contemporaries, like Albert Einstein, was the disparity in the volume of their published work. Einstein, a prolific writer, authored over 300 papers and numerous books, securing a place as a towering figure in theoretical physics. Oppenheimer, on the other hand, produced only a handful of papers after World War II, leading to his relatively limited publication record.

Some observers and scholars have highlighted the potential significance of Oppenheimer's work on gravitational collapse, a subject that could have warranted a Nobel Prize in its own right. This work held implications for our understanding of astrophysical phenomena, yet it remained part of a broader spectrum of contributions that, while important, did not stand out as a singular achievement, which Nobel Prizes are based on.

Though, the essence of Oppenheimer's contribution lay not only in isolated breakthroughs but in his capacity to orchestrate and lead collaborative scientific endeavors. He was someone who carried out his role as director of the Los Alamos Laboratory like a leader, marshaling those who worked with him and bringing out the best in them in the shadow of a project that had never been seriously contemplated before, much less attempted. It was a project that had no blueprint, no failures to learn from or tricks to make things easier. It was a brand new, uncharted, alien endeavor. One which Oppenheimer tied together.

Despite the absence of a Nobel Prize, Oppenheimer's legacy continues to be celebrated by the scientific community and beyond, and perhaps one daresay that his contributions to science and the way he approached it cannot be summed up in any prize.

Nevertheless, the global recognition he received showcased the acknowledgment of his far-reaching influence. And the intellectual atmosphere he fostered, his visionary leadership, and his interdisciplinary approach resonated through generations of scientists and thinkers.

Conclusion

"Winning the prize wasn't half as exciting as doing the work itself."
Maria Goeppert-Mayer

In the annals of scientific inquiry, certain figures emerge as celestial beacons—guiding lights that illuminate uncharted realms of knowledge. J. Robert Oppenheimer was one such luminary, a mind whose brilliance and passion for discovery cast a profound influence on the landscape of physics, transforming our understanding of the universe and of existence itself.

Long before the curtain rose on the monumental drama of the Manhattan Project, Oppenheimer was already a prominent figure in the scientific tapestry. His early years were marked by a relentless pursuit of intellectual horizons, his keen mind thirsting for the secrets of the universe. And his contributions were far greater than the nuclear bomb, and certainly not his only.

As a theoretical physicist, Oppenheimer's work was marked by a deep exploration of the quantum world—a world where particles danced in probabilistic splendor, defying classical intuitions. His journey into the realm of quantum mechanics mirrored the era's fervor for unveiling the mysteries that lay beneath the surface of reality, and every step he took was breaking new ground in a new world that was rapidly challenging old assumptions.

Oppenheimer's theoretical insights not only illuminate the path through the complexities of the microcosmic universe but also ignited discussions that rippled through academic circles. His work resonated as a symphony of ideas, a harmony between theoretical elegance and experimental implications. His engagement with quantum field theory, the theoretical framework that unified the realms of particles and fields, showcased his knack for connecting seemingly disparate concepts.

In this pre-Manhattan Project phase of his career, Oppenheimer stood as a beacon of innovation, challenging the status quo with every equation he penned and every hypothesis he proposed. His role as an educator further cemented his influence, as he imparted his passion for learning and truth-seeking and knowledge to aspiring physicists who would go on to shape the future of science.

From the captivating realm of theoretical physics to the enigmatic world of quantum mechanics, Oppenheimer's groundbreaking discoveries in everything from the study of the atom with the Born-Oppenheimer Approximation to that of nuclear fusion with the heart of our star and all other stars, his wide array of contributions poetically mirrored his uniquely multifaceted nature.

Oppenheimer's collaborations were not only limited to equations, however. They were philosophical dialogues that transcended the confines of laboratories. In vibrant discussions with luminaries like Max Born and Enrico Fermi, Oppenheimer delved into the philosophical implications of quantum mechanics. The nature of reality, the paradoxes of uncertainty, and the interplay between observation and the observed were grist for these intellectual millstones, shaping the very philosophical foundations of modern physics.

The Luminary's Legacy: Shaping Science Education

Oppenheimer was more than just a brilliant physicist; he was a visionary who recognized the pivotal role of science education in shaping the future. His influence on science education in the United States was profound and far-reaching, leaving an indelible mark on generations of aspiring scientists.

Oppenheimer's commitment to nurturing scientific talent was evident throughout his career. He firmly believed that a strong foundation in science education was essential for the advancement of knowledge and the betterment of society. His experiences as an educator and a student had a profound impact on this conviction.

Oppenheimer's time studying under the renowned physicist Max Born in Germany and had developed a deep appreciation for the rigorous scientific education provided by European institutions. This experience fueled his dedication to elevating science education standards in his own home of the United States.

One of the key arenas where Oppenheimer's influence shone was at the University of California, Berkeley, where he served as a professor and head of the Department of Physics. During his tenure, he worked tirelessly to create an environment conducive to scientific excellence. He attracted top-notch faculty, fostered collaborative research, and encouraged a culture of inquiry among students. Many of his students and colleagues from this period would go on to become eminent physicists themselves, a testament to his mentoring and leadership.

Oppenheimer's commitment to science education extended beyond the confines of academia. He was a strong advocate for making scientific knowledge more accessible. He believed that a scientifically literate society was better equipped to make informed decisions about complex scientific and technological issues.

His involvement in educational initiatives was not limited to the university level. Oppenheimer played a pivotal role in the formation of the Educational Testing Service, or ETS, an organization that aimed to improve the assessment of educational achievement. This initiative was a reflection of his desire to promote educational excellence and ensure that educational standards were grounded in rigorous, scientific principles.

Furthermore, Oppenheimer was instrumental in the creation of the Woods Hole Oceanographic Institution, or WHOI, which became a renowned center for marine research and education. His vision for WHOI was to advance the understanding of the oceans through interdisciplinary research and education, fostering a new generation of oceanographers and marine scientists.

Together with all this, he was director of the Institute for Advanced Study in Princeton, where he worked with other luminaries such as Albert Einstein, fostered an environment of intellectual ferment, where brilliant minds converged to explore uncharted territories.

This brings our attention to the National Science Foundation, one of the most important educational institutions of America today that supports learning and research in science and engineering. While Oppenheimer was not a founding member of the NSF, he was at the forefront of discussions that led to its establishment. The post-World War II era was a time of immense scientific discovery and a growing awareness of the pivotal role that science would play in shaping the future, and

Oppenheimer strongly believed that science should be accessible to everyone.

Oppenheimer's journey into the realm of science policy and the NSF began with his recognition of the critical need for government support in advancing scientific research. Having witnessed the unparalleled potential of science, particularly in the fields of nuclear physics and atomic energy, especially its peaceful applications in energy and the like, he believed that the United States should harness this potential through organized and sustained funding.

With the Second World War over, which had demanded the attention of many scientists in the development of radar, penicillin and computers, all geared towards the Allied effort, many, including Oppenheimer, were now transitioning from wartime research to peacetime pursuits while pondering the implications of atomic energy for society. As mentioned earlier, Oppenheimer was acutely aware of the moral, ethical, and strategic dimensions of scientific research, especially in the context of nuclear weapons, and spent his time after the war pushing for nuclear restraint and science education.

Oppenheimer believed that the pursuit of knowledge should not be confined to the private sector or the whims of individual philanthropists. Instead, he argued that the federal government had a responsibility to foster scientific progress and innovation for the betterment of society.

His views resonated with like-minded scientists and policymakers who saw the need for a coordinated and comprehensive approach to scientific research. This led, in 1950, to the establishment of the National Science Foundation. The NSF's mission was and is to promote scientific progress, prosperity, welfare, to improve national health and secure national defense through grants and cooperative agreements supporting research and education across various scientific disciplines.

While Oppenheimer's direct involvement in the creation of the NSF may have been limited, his ideas about the vital role of government support for scientific research were a catalyst for change. The NSF would go on to become a cornerstone of American scientific innovation, providing critical funding for countless scientific endeavors and contributing significantly to the advancement of knowledge.

In retrospect, Oppenheimer's advocacy for the government's role in scientific research underscored the profound relationship between science, government, and society. His ideas laid the groundwork for an enduring legacy of federal support for scientific discovery and innovation, ensuring that the United States remained at the forefront of scientific achievement for decades to come.

With all this, we see that J. Robert Oppenheimer's influence on science education in the United States was profound and multifaceted. His commitment to rigorous scientific training, mentoring of students, and advocacy for educational excellence left an enduring legacy. Oppenheimer's vision for science education as a cornerstone of societal progress continues to inspire educators and scientists to this day, ensuring that future generations of scientists are well-prepared to tackle the challenges of an ever-evolving world.

A Moral Imperative: Scientists as Guardians of Wisdom

As an issue of an equal importance to Oppenheimer as scientific education, the imperative for ethical responsibility to be part of the scientific world and considered together with scientific progress - not as a limitation, but as a humanist guideline, was evident throughout much of his post-Manhattan Project career.

In the tumultuous years following World War II, Oppenheimer emerged as a prominent voice advocating for a profound shift in the role of scientists in society. His experiences as the director of the Los Alamos Laboratory during the Manhattan Project had given him unique insights into the world-changing potential of scientific discoveries, especially in the realm of nuclear technology.

Oppenheimer firmly believed that scientists held a moral responsibility to engage with and advise the government on matters of science and technology, particularly those with profound societal implications. This conviction was born out of a deep recognition of the dual nature of scientific knowledge – a double-edged sword that could either illuminate the path to progress or plunge humanity into darkness. He hoped to make sure the former stayed true.

In the wake of Hiroshima and Nagasaki, Oppenheimer grappled with the realization that the fruits of scientific inquiry could be wielded as instruments of mass destruction. It was a sobering awakening that compelled him to advocate for greater involvement of scientists in matters of national and global significance.

Oppenheimer's vision extended beyond the notion of scientists merely pursuing their research in isolation from the affairs of the world. He saw the need for a balanced relationship between science, government, and society – a relationship built on transparency, accountability, and ethical considerations.

He recognized that runaway scientific advancement, specifically in the field of nuclear technology, had the potential to destabilize the delicate balance of global power. The horrors of nuclear warfare had shattered any illusions of invincibility, leading Oppenheimer to call for responsible scientific progress.

For Oppenheimer, the role of the scientist extended beyond the laboratory; it encompassed active engagement with policymakers and the public. He argued that scientists should provide not just technical expertise but also ethical guidance. They should act as stewards of knowledge, advocating for its responsible use and mitigating its destructive potential. Science, he firmly believed, ought to be peaceful and constructive.

In this endeavor, Oppenheimer became a vocal advocate for international control of atomic energy. His contributions to the Acheson-Lilienthal Report, as mentioned earlier, which proposed a comprehensive plan for the international control of atomic energy, and in the development of the Atoms for Peace initiative to bring light through nuclear power rather than fire and darkness demonstrated his commitment to forging a path toward global security through scientific and ethics-based diplomacy.

Oppenheimer's belief in the moral responsibility of scientists to engage with and advise the government on matters of science and technology was deeply rooted in his experiences and the recognition of the far-reaching consequences of scientific discoveries. He championed the idea that scientists should not be passive observers but active participants in shaping the responsible use of their own creations. His legacy continues to serve as a reminder of the delicate balance that must be struck between scientific progress and its ethical implications in a world where science, government, and society intersect.

The examples he sent as a scientist and frankly, as a person, a member of the human species, were adopted and carried on by the many students and colleagues who had had the privilege of working with him as they disseminated his principles of rigorous scientific inquiry, ethical conduct, and the responsible use of scientific knowledge across academia, research, and government service.

Oppenheimer's influence permeated the scientific community, shaping the values and aspirations of those who followed in his footsteps. His dedication to the responsible use of scientific discoveries, particularly in the context of nuclear technology, left an indelible mark. His leadership in the Manhattan Project was a crucible that forged not just atomic weapons but also a cadre of scientists committed to the betterment of humanity.

In the end, J. Robert Oppenheimer's iconic stature in the field of nuclear physics and his enduring impact on the broader scientific community were a testament to the confluence of brilliance, leadership, and moral conviction. He was more than a scientist; he was a torchbearer of scientific ethics and a beacon for generations of scientists who sought to balance the pursuit of knowledge with the responsibility of its consequences.

Oppenheimer's Many Scientific Contributions

It is thus undoubtedly clear that the tapestry of Oppenheimer's contributions was rich with nuance and depth—a testament to his unyielding curiosity and collaborative spirit. His theories and collaborations transcended the theoretical realm, breathing life into practical applications that transformed industries, deepened our understanding of the cosmos, and ignited philosophical discourse. As he navigated the intricate corridors of the quantum world, Oppenheimer wove a narrative of brilliance, collaboration, and a thirst for understanding that would continue to resonate through the corridors of scientific thought for generations to come.

In the cosmic theater of theoretical physics, J. Robert Oppenheimer's intellectual odyssey took him to the furthest reaches of space and time, on scales far opposite that of the quantum realm, where the gravitational embrace of black holes and the enigmatic realm of neutron stars awaited his probing mind. These celestial enigmas, shrouded in mystery, became the focus of Oppenheimer's quest to unravel the secrets of the cosmos.

Collaborating with Hartland Snyder, Oppenheimer delved into the fate of massive stars that had exhausted their nuclear fuel. Their landmark paper, aptly titled "On Continued Gravitational Contraction," and published in 1939, laid the foundations for understanding the collapse of massive stars under their own gravity.

They posited that the energy produced in the fiery core of a massive star, allowing it to shine brightly, created by the fusion of atoms deep within it, pushes outward against the relentless pull of gravity that seeks to compress the star's matter. For a long time, these opposing forces maintain a delicate balance, and the star remains stable.

However, Oppenheimer and Snyder explored what happens when this balance is disrupted. Once its nuclear fuel is depleted, with no energy left to counteract gravity's pull, the star embarks on a journey of contraction—a process where it gradually shrinks under the immense weight of its own matter.

As the star contracts, a breathtaking transformation unfolds. The core becomes denser, and the star's gravity grows stronger. It's like a cosmic version of a squeezed balloon, but on a cosmic scale. Oppenheimer and Snyder's work revealed a critical moment in this process—a point where the star's contraction becomes unstoppable.

At this juncture, the star crosses a cosmic threshold known as the Chandrasekhar limit, named after another brilliant scientist Subrahmanyan Chandrasekhar. Beyond this limit, no force can halt the star's collapse, and it plunges into a dramatic transformation. The outer layers cascade inward at astonishing speeds, hurtling toward the core with a momentum that defies imagination, allowing a singularity to emerge.

The paper's significance rests in its insight into what happens when this unstoppable collapse leads to the creation of a black hole. Oppenheimer's and Snyder's calculations unveilved the event horizon, a boundary beyond which nothing can escape the black hole—not even light itself. This event horizon marks the point of no return, a boundary that shapes the eerie silhouette of a black hole against the cosmic canvas.

This groundbreaking insight into the nature of black holes would later become a cornerstone of astrophysics and reshape our understanding of the universe's most enigmatic phenomena.

Yet, Oppenheimer's exploration didn't stop at black holes. His insatiable curiosity drew him toward another celestial puzzle: neutron stars. Collaborating with George Volkoff, Oppenheimer delved into the exotic realm where matter was compressed to unimaginable densities, resulting in stars composed almost entirely of neutrons, shining blue and burning several times hotter than our own sun.

Oppenheimer and Volkoff's work, now known as the Oppenheimer-Volkoff limit, established a critical threshold beyond which the pull of gravity was so immense that even atomic nuclei could no longer withstand collapse. This landmark theoretical insight unveiled the upper mass limit for neutron stars, just as the Chandrasekhar limit did for dwarf stars, marking the boundary between these enigmatic objects and the gravitational abyss of black holes.

The significance of Oppenheimer's work on black holes and neutron stars extended beyond theoretical physics, resonating within the pulsars and quasars that dotted the cosmic landscape. His theoretical underpinnings illuminated the mechanics behind these cosmic powerhouses, offering insights into the fundamental forces and processes that drove their behavior.

These pursuits required not only a good grasp of equations and theorems but also an imaginative leap into realms where the laws of nature were stretched to their limits, and where little to no understanding existed. As a theoretical visionary, Oppenheimer's work laid the groundwork for generations of astrophysicists who would follow in his footsteps, seeking to decipher the symphony of forces that govern the universe's most captivating phenomena.

In the vast landscape of theoretical physics, where particles and fields dance in intricate harmony, J. Robert Oppenheimer cast a luminous spotlight on a groundbreaking framework that would revolutionize our understanding of the universe through quantum field theory, or QFT. As a visionary thinker, his journey into the realm of QFT would weave together the symphony of particles, fields, and interactions.

Oppenheimer's foray into this field was not a solitary endeavor—it was a harmonious collaboration with fellow physicists, a collective effort that resonated with the spirit of scientific exploration. This expedition led to the development of a novel approach known as the Oppenheimer-Phillips Process, which we saw earlier in the book, providing a mathematical framework to understand the phenomenon of quantum tunneling—an intricate dance where particles surmount energy barriers that in classical physics, should be insurmountable.

Together with its implications for how matter could be manipulated at the molecular level, the Process also held profound implications for nuclear physics, elucidating how particles, driven by the probabilistic nature of quantum mechanics, could navigate the seemingly forbidden territory of energy states. It was a revelation that transcended mathematical equations; it unveiled the intricate quantum nature of the subatomic world, offering insights into the very heart of the cosmos.

Yet, Oppenheimer's contributions to quantum field theory extended beyond the confines of nuclear reactions. His pioneering spirit intersected with the burgeoning field of particle physics, where QFT emerged as a tool to understand the fundamental forces that shape our universe. Oppenheimer's explorations in this realm paved the way for the unification of electromagnetism and the weak nuclear force—an endeavor that would later be realized in the electroweak theory.

Another one of his pivotal contributions was his exploration of renormalization—a mathematical technique that reconciles the infinities that arise in quantum field theory calculations. Through this intricate dance of mathematical finesse, Oppenheimer paved the way for QFT to accurately predict physical outcomes without succumbing to divergent mathematical results. This elegant solution demonstrated his ability to navigate the complexities of theory, ensuring that QFT remained a potent and reliable tool for understanding the subatomic world.

As Oppenheimer navigated the labyrinthine pathways of QFT, he bridged the gap between theoretical elegance and experimental implications. His collaborations and insights extended far beyond the equations, shaping the very foundations of quantum field theory. And he engaged not only with particles and fields, but also with the philosophical underpinnings of this revolutionary framework, pondering the implications of its probabilistic nature on our understanding of reality.

In the intricate mosaic of quantum field theory, Oppenheimer's contributions were brushstrokes of brilliance. His explorations into the quantum realm illuminated the subtle interplay of particles, the dance of probabilities, and the fusion of his scientific knowledge and profound insight. Through his tireless efforts, Oppenheimer left an indelible mark on quantum field theory, enriching the tapestry of human understanding and paving the way for generations of physicists to unravel the mysteries of the cosmos.

Oppenheimer's impact on nuclear physics was not confined to equations alone; it extended to our very perception of reality. His research illuminated the fundamental interplay between particles, forces, and energy, painting a vivid portrait of the building blocks of matter and the intricate dance that unfolds within the atomic nucleus.

As Oppenheimer navigated the realms of nuclear physics, he catalyzed a shift in our understanding of the universe's building blocks. His insights enriched our comprehension of the forces that govern the atomic world, from the subtle interactions between quarks and gluons to the explosive dynamics of nuclear reactions.

Ironically, for all the brilliance that radiated from J. Robert Oppenheimer's mind, an intriguing paradox emerged—one that often escapes the spotlight. Oppenheimer's mental landscape was a tapestry of paradoxes. As a theoretical visionary, he wove equations that unraveled the mysteries of the quantum realm, reshaping our understanding of reality. His collaborations with fellow luminaries illuminated the nature of particles, fields, and the cosmos itself. Yet, in the realm of everyday numbers and calculations, he stumbled.

This quirk of his intellectual makeup, while often overshadowed by his groundbreaking contributions, adds a touch of humanity to his towering stature. It reminds us that brilliance is multifaceted—a constellation of strengths and idiosyncrasies. Oppenheimer's inability to master arithmetic didn't deter his exploration of the universe's deepest secrets, and to us, it underscores the intricate diversity that makes up the spectrum of human intelligence.

His limitations in arithmetic serve as a reminder that scientific genius can manifest in myriad ways. The intricate dance of theoretical physics and the calculations of daily life are distinct arenas, each testing different cognitive faculties. Oppenheimer's story encourages us to embrace the complexities within ourselves, recognizing that brilliance transcends conventional definitions and flourishes in unexpected corners of our minds.

As the annals of history recount Oppenheimer's contributions, this lesser-known facet adds depth to his narrative—a reminder that the journey of intellectual discovery is often a complex tapestry woven from threads of various skills and insights. In celebrating his scientific achievements, we also celebrate the unique symphony that is each individual's intellectual journey.

In considering Julius Robert Oppenheimer's impact on the course of scientific progress and human development, we turn to his efforts in the development of the atomic bomb and the prospects, terrible and awesome that it ushered in, as well as the aftermath of the Second World War, the most devastating conflict in human history, when he worked to guide and temper the growth of nuclear power. His post-war contributions would transcend equations and laboratories, leaving an indelible mark on the collaborative spirit that fuels scientific progress, his influence extending into the realms of science, policy and international cooperation. In a world scarred by the scourge of war, he recognized the profound potential of science to foster unity and understanding.

J. Robert Oppenheimer in Popular Culture: A Multi-Faceted Portrait

As the linchpin of the Manhattan Project, the ambitious endeavor that birthed the atomic bomb - though he did so much more than that, his life and legacy have captivated the imagination of writers, filmmakers, and documentarians alike. The portrayal of Oppenheimer in popular culture is thus a testament to the complex tapestry of his existence.

The literary realm stands as a rich repository of Oppenheimer's legacy. Scores of books have meticulously chronicled his life, offering readers diverse perspectives on his contributions and character. Foremost among these is "American Prometheus: The Triumph and Tragedy of J. Robert Oppenheimer" by Kai Bird and Martin J. Sherwin. This magnum opus not only garnered the Pulitzer Prize for Biography or Autobiography but also etched Oppenheimer's journey into the public consciousness.

Within the pages of these books, readers dive into the intricate interplay of Oppenheimer's scientific achievements, his vital part in the Manhattan Project, and the controversies that encircled his career. They navigate the labyrinth of his mind, his ethical struggles, and his shifting stance on the moral implications of atomic weaponry. The written word thus becomes a portal through which Oppenheimer's life unfolds, a captivating narrative that invites contemplation.

If books serve as a chronicle, films are the moving canvas upon which Oppenheimer's life and the moral quandaries of the atomic age are painted. The silver screen has rendered his character in vivid hues, capturing the essence of his complexity. In "*Fat Man and Little Boy*" (1989), audiences are transported to the heart of the Manhattan Project, where they bear witness to the clash of scientific ambition and moral reckoning. "*The Day After Trinity*" (1981) provides another lens, peering into the ethical complexities of the era, casting Oppenheimer as a central figure in the moral drama of the atomic age.

Through the cinematic lens, Oppenheimer becomes more than a historical figure; he becomes a relatable human being grappling with the monumental consequences of his scientific endeavors. His character transcends the pages of history books, his moral dilemmas etched onto the celluloid canvas.

For those who seek a deeper exploration of Oppenheimer's life and its controversies, documentaries stand as a compelling medium. Works such as "*The Trials of J. Robert Oppenheimer*" (2008) and "*J. Robert Oppenheimer: Father of the Atomic Bomb*" (2017) undertake an exhaustive examination of his journey. They feature interviews with historians, colleagues, and experts, offering a multi-dimensional view of his legacy.

In these documentaries, Oppenheimer's life and its complexities are unveiled layer by layer. His ethical struggles, his inner turmoil, and his evolving perspectives are scrutinized, allowing viewers to contemplate the man behind the science. The fusion of historical footage, expert insights, and personal narratives fashions a nuanced portrayal that is both intellectually stimulating and emotionally resonant.

In popular culture, J. Robert Oppenheimer emerges not as a one-dimensional figure but as a multi-faceted and enduring presence. Books, films, and documentaries stand as diverse canvases, each rendering a distinct facet of his life and the moral questions that continue to reverberate through the ages. The examination of

Oppenheimer in popular culture serves as an invitation to delve deeper into the complex interplay of science, ethics, and the human condition.

A Tapestry of Interpretation and Myth

It is clear from this that Oppenheimer has been many times woven into the rich tapestry of interpretation and mythologization, each with different ever-evolving narratives, spurred again now in the 21st century by ponderous epics such as Christopher Nolan's *Oppenheimer*, all reflecting shifting perspectives on science, politics, and the tumultuous atomic age that defined Oppenheimer's era.

Like a chameleon, Oppenheimer has assumed different guises in the theater of interpretation. To some, he stands as a resolute hero, his leadership in the Manhattan Project celebrated as a pivotal contribution to the triumph of the Allied forces in World War II. His brilliance and unwavering commitment to harnessing atomic energy for the greater good are cast in a heroic light.

Yet, the same figure dons a cloak of tragedy. His later struggles, entangled in the web of government security clearances and his piercing questioning of the use of atomic weapons, paint him as a tragic figure. The fervor with which he once pursued scientific progress becomes tinged with remorse. Oppenheimer's transformation from a brilliant scientist to a man haunted by the shadows of the atomic age serves as a stark reminder of the moral complexities of the era.

The ethical crucible in which Oppenheimer's life unfolded has also inspired a kaleidoscope of interpretations. Some view him as a principled scientist who grappled earnestly with the moral consequences of his work. They argue that his ethical awakening, his recognition of the destructive potential of atomic weaponry, and his advocacy for international control were emblematic of a deeply principled man burdened by the weight of knowledge.

Conversely, others do not shy away from critiquing Oppenheimer's initial enthusiasm for atomic weapons. They see his remorse and later moral reservations as too little, too late, and the moral dilemmas that define his narrative are perceived not as a path of redemption but as an indelible stain on his legacy.

In the arena of interpretation which has attracted much debate, it is clear that Oppenheimer's legacy is a complicated one, with multiple perspectives and angles to consider, many of them valid at the same time, even if they sound contradictory. This suits the fact that Oppenheimer is not a monolith; he is a multi-faceted enigma. Analysts and scholars have revealed his complexity, portraying him as a brilliant scientist, a charismatic leader, and a profoundly controversial figure. His life story unfolds like a Greek tragedy, with moments of triumph and moments of hubris. His charisma captivated colleagues and the public alike, yet his actions sparked controversy and governmental scrutiny.

Oppenheimer's enigmatic character invites interpretation and debate. He embodies the intricate interplay of intellect and morality, ambition and remorse, leadership and doubt. His complexities beckon scholars and storytellers to plumb the depths of his persona, uncovering layers of meaning and shedding light on the moral and ethical questions that resonate through the ages.

In the annals of history, J. Robert Oppenheimer is not just a man; he is a narrative, a symbol, and an archetype. Interpretations and mythologizations of his life and work continue to evolve, providing a mirror to our changing attitudes toward science, politics, and the enduring legacy of the atomic age.

At the heart of this discourse lies the profound ethical inquiry into the responsibilities of scientists engaged in groundbreaking, potentially world-altering research. The life of Oppenheimer, with its central role in the creation of the atomic bomb, epitomizes this dilemma. How should society assess the ethical responsibility of scientists like Oppenheimer, whose scientific prowess led to the development of a weapon capable of unparalleled destruction?

The ethical conundrum extends beyond the individual scientist to the collective responsibility of the scientific community and society at large. It challenges us to push the limits of scientific inquiry and to grapple with the moral implications of knowledge. In the case of Oppenheimer, his scientific brilliance was instrumental in the Allied victory during World War II, yet it also unleashed a weapon of mass destruction. The ethical nuances of this dual role continue to resonate, forcing us to reckon with the enduring ethical dilemmas of scientific discovery.

Ethical Evolution

Oppenheimer's evolution from an enthusiastic advocate of atomic weapons to a figure marked by remorse provokes a deeply philosophical and moral debate. Does this transformation reflect commendable ethical growth and/or a belated realization of the catastrophic consequences of his actions? That, of course, is weighed against the knowledge that he lived an ethical life and placed great emphasis on morality and doing good, culminating in a question that is still difficult to definitively answer.

The trajectory of Oppenheimer's ethical awakening serves as a microcosm of broader ethical debates surrounding the use of atomic weaponry. It challenges us to consider whether ethical judgment should be based solely on intentions or also on the ultimate consequences of one's actions. This ethical evolution also raises questions about the individual's capacity for introspection, redemption, and the acknowledgment of moral responsibility in the face of monumental decisions.

Myth vs. Reality

The interplay between myth and historical reality in the portrayal of Oppenheimer beckons us to scrutinize the ethical implications of myth-making. To what extent do the mythologized versions of Oppenheimer's life align with historical reality, and how does this myth-making shape our understanding of his legacy and the ethical judgments we pass?

Myths often serve to simplify complex narratives, transforming individuals into archetypal heroes or villains. In the case of Oppenheimer, the challenge lies in disentangling the myth from the historical record and assessing the ethical consequences of such simplification. The construction of myth can distort our understanding of the moral dilemmas faced by those who shape history through their work, blurring the lines between fact and fiction.

In the end, the portrayals of J. Robert Oppenheimer in popular culture serve as a crucible for enduring ethical and moral inquiries. They compel us to reexamine the ethical responsibilities of scientists, ponder the nature of ethical evolution, and navigate the intricate terrain where myth and reality converge. These questions not only illuminate the legacy of a singular figure but also provide a lens through which we scrutinize the ethical considerations of scientific discovery in the modern world, underscoring the enduring relevance of Oppenheimer's story.

A Human Who Changed History

In the mosaic of his post-war contributions, Oppenheimer emerged as a statesman of science—an advocate for the unity of knowledge, the responsible application of discovery, and the ethical considerations that must guide the course of human progress. His vision of peace and unique idea of progress resonates as a testament to the boundless potential of science to unite humanity under a common purpose. As he navigated the intricate interplay between physics, policy, and ethics, Oppenheimer became a beacon that illuminated not just the realms of atoms and particles, but the very essence of human aspirations for a better, more harmonious world.

Beyond the many realms of physics in which Oppenheimer had changed the world, he was also a philosophical man who valued the intangible as well as the tangible. He was a man who loved to read and hear the diverse perspectives of our diverse world, to see the bits of truth that everyone has to offer, all adding to the grand tapestry of life's truth. He found wisdom in the ancient Western classics and the Eastern texts. His childhood was defined by an emphasis on humanity, dignity, justice, and ethics, and all of this came together to create a person with the utmost awareness.

Oppenheimer understood science with the grace of philosophy and faith, and understood them in the bright light that science casts on our world and its most fundamental building blocks. He was a layered, complex, but not complicated man, who also cared deeply for the people in his life as much, if not more, than his work, which he truly loved.

His life was full of ironies and contradictions and untenable situations that he always navigated with a collected calm. Neither cold nor aloof, but rational and level. Even his battles with depression and erratic, sometimes overly aggressive behavior during his younger years were part of the dichotomy of his nature as a kind and caring soul.

In light of all this, seeing Oppenheimer as a man who read as enthusiastically as he penned groundbreaking concepts, who was as strongly compassionate as he was sometimes strongly arrogant and abrasive, it is no surprise that Oppenheimer also faced the most conflicting task in history in the development of the atomic bomb, faced with the choice between the horrors of a nuclear Nazi regime and the lesser horror of an Allied nuclear weapon.

It is thus clear that Oppenheimer's legacy in the pages of physics is not merely a historical footnote—it's a dynamic force that reverberates through time that changed the world on a greater scale than many who have been able to claim that role did.

He set the stage for all those who followed after him, with his unparalleled work in quantum mechanics, nuclear physics, and quantum field theory, offering a springboard for innovative thinking and discovery like never before.

In the panorama of science, life, and existence, Oppenheimer's legacy shines not merely as a compendium of theories, but as an embodiment of the human spirit's quest for knowledge. His impact is imprinted not just in equations but in the very fabric of scientific endeavor, where each question asked, each boundary pushed, with an important emphasis on humanity and ethics, is a continuation of the journey he embarked upon—a journey that transcends time, guiding us toward an ever-deeper understanding of the cosmos we call home.

And rightfully so, as of December 16th, 2022, J. Robert Oppenheimer's reputation, which had been blemished by the McCarthy era, now stands completely restored. The mistakes made in the tragedy that befell him have been thoroughly recognized with the US government's decision to overturn the revocation of his security clearance, voiding the initial decision.

Made in United States
Orlando, FL
23 March 2024